KILL HIM!! KILL HIM!! TI as I stood over him pointing the barrel of the .22 ca... ectly at his temple. He was still asleep, so I pressed down a little harder trying to wake him up so he could look into my eyes before I ended his miserable life. As he opened his beady, little eyes and tried to focus, it seemed as if time stood completely still for that short moment. I could see every single dust particle floating around the room in slow motion. The scent of his morning breathe resonated throughout the air as he screamed "NO...PLEASE....WAIT!!" and begged for his life.

KILL HIM!! KILL HIM!! The voices were running rampant in my head... KILL HIM!!

All of a sudden, a sense of calm washed all over my body as my finger started to pull down on the trigger....

It's funny how life has its way of changing you.

Looking back, it is painfully obvious that my childhood was EVERYTHING BUT NORMAL. Unable to remember even a handful of happy memories is the first clue. Only memories of pain, tears, grief and suffering is what has been etched into my brain for so many years. Such dreadfully engorged memories, still to this day, causes me to suffer from terrors of the hellish nightmare I called life.

Throughout my life, everyone has always felt the need to chime in with their two cents about how they could imagine and fantasize of how great it must be to be the child of a famous celebrity and how blessed I am. With being in the limelight, big fancy houses, luxury cars, and trips around the world; not to mention shopping sprees and lobster dinners with all of the bells and whistles included, it must be a dream. Oh yea, it SOUNDS nice... but sometimes you have to look a little deeper than what you see on the surface.

Being the daughter of a National Basketball Association (NBA) record holder and Hall of Famer, one would think that I should automatically have natural bragging rights, but unfortunately the truth is, it is a curse and I tried to hide my true identity from the world even as an adult. And since it literally makes me sick to my stomach to call this monster my father, I will be referring to him as C.M.

Just because C.M. was my biological father, we were never apart of a REAL family. You see, my mother was one of C.M.'s side pieces' (a mistress) for over 25 years and my sisters, bother and I, the Love Children, where known as the little unwanted, mixed bastards.
Everyone's family tree isn't so simple; mine is more like a bush with thrones.

I guess it wasn't bad enough that we were the forbidden children of this famous, black married celebrity, but we also just so happened to be the children of a young, white country girl 12 years his junior. You can just imagine the drama surrounding this scandal because in the 1980's, due to interracial relationships, in addition to adultery, being highly frowned upon by society, not to mention his wife.

My mother had to have some notion of the consequences she would face following the dumb ass decision to become romantically involved and fall in love with a well-known, black, married man. This decision was what would change the course of our lives and dash many hopes and dreams for the future; disappointing many people.
This disappointment would come not only from society, but from the two people that she loved the most, her parents.

Born and raised in the Deep South, Magnolia TX, my mother's Negro hating parents, (my grandparents) were the most racist, strict and demanding couple you could meet.
My grandfather was a tough Pearl Harbor Navy Veteran and my grandmother a sinister, bitter, housewife that lived to care for my grandfather and mother.
They both had big dreams for their daughter. Since my mother was a nationally renowned, award winning painter and pianist since the age of 11, my grandparents knew their daughter was going to make a prestigious name for herself and make them proud. With the best schools and opportunities provided, my mother graduated from High School at the early age of 16 and was granted an Academic Scholarship to Houston Baptist University. She was on her way!!.... My grandparents were so certain that she was going to leave the nest, graduate from college, marry a nice corporate white boy, bare white grandkids

and live happily ever after.
And as you now know, their hopes and dreams came crashing down and in their minds, this evil black man was the cause.

During her very first semester of this newly found freedom called college life, is when my mother meets and falls in love with the monster of her dreams, C.M.

Nowadays with the heightened security and the NBA teams having their own arenas for games, it is very difficult for groupies and gold diggers to make their way to the locker rooms to meet and harass the players, looking for a meal ticket. But in the 1970's, before the luxuries the NBA players have today, the teams were forced to hold practices at one of the black Universities in the area. Low and behold, the Houston Rockets, the team C.M. was a Point Guard for, was designated to practice at my mother's school, Houston Baptist University. Every afternoon the Rockets would be in the school's gym working out for hours at a time. Being the team's athletic department's assistant for her work-study program, my mother had continuous, unsupervised interaction with the guys on all of the teams. While performing one duties to deliver water, towels and equipment to the practicing team, the Houston Rockets, is the moment her entire life changed forever; the beginning of her demise.

Once C.M. laid his eyes on this young, naïve, teenage white girl, he knew he had fresh meat and pounced on his chance to get her in his grasp. Star struck, my mother fell for every word, every pick up line and all the other bullshit lies he fed her to gain her trust. But one thing I'm sure he failed to mention in his mission capture another soul, was that he was married with children. Obviously, this little bit of information didn't deter my mother from pursuing and locking down a relationship with this man.

Having to look over her shoulder constantly, hide their relationship, sneak around, be with each other during late night hours, and try cover their every step to be certain no one saw them, became the norm for her. He told her if word got out, it would be all over news and would ruin his marriage, reputation and his career; so in order to keep her man happy, she did exactly what C.M. told her to do, hide. Hide from society, family and the world to keep our identity a secret.

ANGELLE' DAVIDSON

    We were forced to move from place to place every few months and live in rat and roach infested motels and run down apartments in the worse areas of Houston, TX. We would come home to thugs and homeless people breaking into our small efficiency apartment, stealing the little bit of food that we did have and anything else that they thought was of benefit.

    On a few occasions, the person that broke into our home wasn't even someone from the streets, instead it would be one of C.M's other side pieces that had followed us home.

    There was this crazy ass woman actually creeping around our apartment one night in the dark waiting for my mother to step in the door. My siblings and I were walking a few feet behind our mother, when she unlocked the front door, stepped in preparing to turn on the lights as she usually would and then all of a sudden, we heard an unknown voice from within out apartment scream "BITCH"!!, followed by a loud, glass shattering crash. My brother was the first one of us to make it to the front door just to see our mother tousling around on the ground, bloody, trying to gouge this chic's eyes out of her skull. Furniture was breaking, glass and picture frames were flying, smashing into the walls, it was the WWE in the middle of our living room.

Of course, as a little kid, I was terrified and didn't know what to do, so naturally I started to scream to the top of my lungs for help. My brother and sisters were a little older so they were down to fight and rushed in to help my mother defeat this psycho, kicking and hitting her with whatever they could get their hands on. What seemed like forever was about a 30 min. confrontation before the cops made it to the scene. And only after the cops arrived and put the lady into cuffs did we find out who this lady really was…C.M.'s wife!

    A few weeks before the attack, we were aware that someone was targeting my mother, but with my young age, I had no idea why. Her car tires would be slashed in the middle of the night and/or windows busted out. Death threats would be left on our door and continuous phone calls at all hours of the day and night with just someone breathing on the other end. Things were getting very weird and dangerous.

At one point, we weren't even allowed to go outside or even look out of the window in fear of another attack from C.M's wife or one of the many other women that he was involved with. We lived in constant fear for our lives.

This mayhem explains why my mother took such extreme measures to try and hide our location and identity from the world regardless what horrible sacrifices we had to make.
During the early years of our lives, my siblings and I were literally forbidden to speak to anyone about the fact that we knew C.M. and most definitely couldn't relinquish the fact that he was our father. Him being our father was hidden better than any government classified UFO file and we knew if one word was spoken about him being around or even if we slipped up and told someone that he was our father, he would beat the living hell out of us so bad that we would be left scared and battered, unable to sit down or even walk for days.

C.M. was most definitely not the loving, caring, affectionate person and father he disguised himself to be in the public's eye. Oh Hell NO! On the contrary, he was the absolute opposite. With anything that he found unsatisfactory, let it be something we said, a face we made, if we were talking too much or if he was just in a bad mood and we were around; no matter how minor it may have been, would give him justification to take a branch off of the nearest tree, grab a wire hanger nearby or belt, so he could relentlessly beat us. Thrash after thrash... he wouldn't stop until he drew blood from our torn flesh or until he hit us so hard that his Hall of Fame belt buckle would lodged into the flesh of our back and get stuck between the bloody tissue and muscle.
A trip to the Emergency room was always urgently necessary, immediately after our punishment to stich or staple the gashes on our legs and arms or back, closed.
Because of this, in the midst of summer in Houston, with a minimum of 100 degrees outside, in the shade, we were forced to wear long sleeve shirts and Jeans wherever we went to hide the bruises, stiches or any other evidence of the abuse that was visible. Immediately, we were readily prepared with a script of excuses to tell anyone that would happen to see the deep purple and blue marks and become curious. The words, "I hurt myself playing basketball" or "an accident

while playing outside" was drilled into my head so much, it became a natural response to any injury I had, regardless of what may have truly happened.

I bet you are wondering how and why did my mother let this happen. You see, that is a question I have asked myself for a very long time now. WHY??!! WHY??!! WHY??!! Did she love him more than she loved her kids? Did she not love us at all?

The sad truth is that my mother was a very mentally weak woman that world revolved around this horrible man and in order to keep him, she allowed him to do any and everything he wanted to do to her and to us. So easily manipulated and controlled, he had her brainwashed and underneath his black achy thumb. Her only response to the abuse we endured, was to sit in the next room listening to the excruciating screams of her young children being brutally beaten, and cry. She wouldn't dare attempt to speak up or even stop the beatings or save us from being tortured. She just stood by, did absolutely nothing and cried.

Once the torture was finally over, each time without fail, my mother would take us from C.M.'s house of hell, then take us to Dairy Queen for ice cream and try to console and nurture us excessively, as if she was trying to make up for allowing it to happen. Trying to make it seem like she actually cared with those all too familiar crocodile tears running down her pasty white and red cheeks. We witnessed those exact same useless crocodile tears each time we were abused and beaten, when she just sat back and did nothing.

Devastatingly enough, the beatings and physical abuse wasn't the only horrible treatment we had to endure. It seemed like my mother never felt that we deserved any better than the tormented reality we were living in and it most definitively showed.

With my mother using food as a coping mechanism for the abuse she was subjecting us to, you can just imagine how I grew to become a very robust kid. I was wearing Plus Sized Woman's clothing by time I was in the 4th grade. My brother and I were called the M & M Twins growing up; even though we were 3 years apart. We were BIG! With that, needless to say, I was at the center of C.M.'s ridicule at every chance he got and I felt every ounce of his constant humiliating jokes and banter directed at me and my size whenever I was in his presence.

Regardless of what public place we may have been visiting while traveling with C.M., without hesitation he would make it his mission to inform the entire establishment of how fat I was.

One of the most embarrassing moments in my life that has help mold my insecurities: C.M. allowed my mother, siblings and I to accompany him and his entourage to dinner at a well-known buffet restaurant in the city. Having a packed house that night, the Manager seated us at the biggest table, smack dead in the middle of the room. Even though, initially, I had reservations about going to dinner because C.M. would be present, I made the biggest mistake and decided to go. Usually, I would beg my mother to allow me stay home when she had plans to meet up with him, but this time my chubby ass could only think about all the delicious food that was going to be at my fingertips. Also, figuring that since C.M.'s friends would be with us as a group, I assumed he would put on that fake facade of him being a decent person and hide who is truly was.

Well, SURPRISE, SURPRISE… true colors always show. After the entire table came back from the buffet counter with their plates, sat down and prepared to eat, C.M. stood at the head of the table to announce to the entire restaurant that I had put too much food on my plate. "That's why you are so God Damn fat now, you fat ass pig!, he aggressively proclaimed in a loud, stern voice. Just loud enough to entice the entire restaurant full of patrons to freeze in mid bite, turn towards our table to see what the commotion was.
Maybe a mere few seconds passed in-between statements, but it felt like hours. I felt all those eyes just burning a hole through me as their feelings of pity and disgust filled the room through the whispers of the ones that actually heard exactly what was said; in disbelief that this highly recognized celebrity was behaving this way.

As the customers slowly began to resume with their own dinners, the Manager casually strolled over, trying not to upset C.M. even further, to ask if everything was alright. Apparently, C.M. hadn't made his point clear because he continued to rant and rave to the Manager

as well as pointing and yelling at my mother to take my plate away from me and I wasn't allowed to finish my meal.
Of course, I didn't say a damn word, but I felt the heat rising from the tip of my toes to the follicles on the top of my head. I dropped my face towards my lap, holding my breath deeply, trying my toughest not to cry. I remember that I held my breath for so long, my face started to turn purple and my eyes felt like they were going to pop out of the sockets. But to no avail, as soon as I gasped for air, the tears started streaming down my plump flushed cheeks uncontrollably. After this asshole witnessed the damage that he had done to this 8 year old little girl, he just sat there with a devilish grin on his face as if he was proud of the traumatizing memory he just created for me and told my mother to "escort me to the restroom until I shut up".
C.M. delivered this type of mental anguish continuously throughout my entire adolescence with various malicious displays of public humiliation.

    The only time I can remember not being publicly chastised by C.M. is when we were in the vicinity of his collogues or business partners. It was like being in a scene of Dr. Jeckel and Mr. Hyde, because he transformed into a completely different person. He all of a sudden became Father of the Year. He would laugh and smile with us, pretending to have a meaningful, loving conversations with his "adoring children" and all the while he processed such demonic tendencies.

    At this time in our lives, C.M. was at the forefront of his popularity due to his position as a national television commentator for the Houston Rockets. His face was plastered all over Houston Billboards and commercials flooded the airwaves promoting this All American, humanitarian and influential role model for kids. We couldn't travel anywhere in Houston without someone stopping him for an autograph or a picture. The kids at our schools would either try to be our best friends to see if they could get any of the perks that might come with our friendship or that would be so jealous and envious they would hate our guts before they knew us personally. No matter what the case may have been, we were the luckiest kids in the world in everyone's eyes. Despite the fact that he was our demon, almost everyone in

Houston and across the U.S. absolutely adored this creep.
With how wonderful our lives were portrayed to be, would anyone think that such an "amazing" man could have a dark, evil side...even worse than the mental abuse and the beatings he would give his children??
Unfortunate for us, things were much worse than any horror story Stephen King could create. This man's dark side is what claimed our innocence, sanity and took us to the point of no return.

Just like most normal siblings, my brother and I would battle each other on a daily bases. Name calling, fist fights and playing annoying pranks on each other was our daily routine. "Dumb ass", "Fat Slob" were just a couple of the loving nicks names that we gave each other. Not one day would pass without my mother losing her temper and yelling at us threatened to "slap the shit out of us" if she heard another word out of us. My brother and I would have been too much for any parent to deal with; we were horrible. Bad attitudes and smart mouths were just a few of our flaws adults had to deal with.

I suppose this one faithful day with my brother and I, claimed to be too much for my mother to handle and she decided to send us to spend the night with C.M. at his house of horror. Of course, I begged and pleaded to for her to reconsider, but to no avail, she made us go anyway. Even though I was merely 6 years old, I remember vividly having such a terrifying, gut wrenching feeling while driving over to Lucifer's slumber party not knowing this was the night my pure spirit would be crushed irreversibly and innocence stolen.

The evening started off without incident. C.M. had a few of his friends over and they were in the game room preoccupied with playing pool and listening to his Oldie's music collection he prided himself on having. After seeing that he had company for the night, I was put at ease and was content knowing that in just a few hours I would be leaving that pit of darkness and be back in the safely of my own home away from him.

The night was winding down and I was in the bathroom preparing for bed. I remember thinking, the sooner I went to sleep, the sooner it would be morning and I could get the hell out of there. I changed out of my school clothes and into my New Kids on the Block nightgown, had a brief intermission with my brother and then off to bed.

On that particular night, for some off reason, C.M. insisted for my brother and me to sleep in his king sized bed, in the master bedroom. Trying not to anger this ticking time bomb, without hesitation we went down the hallway to his room, to settle in for the night.

An hour or so had passed and all was quite throughout the house, so we assumed all the company had departed and C.M. had fell asleep on the couch. This alieved my fear and anxiety of hoping he wouldn't find a reason to come in and beat our ass and we finally dozed off.

Not sure of how much time had passed since I fell sleep or what time of the night or morning it might have been when I heard something or someone on the other side of the closed room door. Initially, I was startled by the creaking sound I was hearing not sure of exactly where it was coming from. I immediately popped straight up in the bed, wide eyed quickly scanning the pitch black bedroom making sure the boogie man wasn't coming to rip me apart or pull me under the bed; the first thoughts of a young child starring into darkness. Minuets went by and the noise subsided so my eyelids started getting heavy once again and I went back to dream world. Creeeeek....Creeeeek....Creeeeek... There it goes again! A little more terrified this time, I just laid there and pulled the blanket over my head feeling the boogie man couldn't find me over there. But to my terror, this time the creaking was followed by the clicking of the door knob turning and a slow, faint squeal caused by the rusty door hinge. Petrified by what might be coming through the door, I tried to shake my brother awake, which was on the far side of the bed, furthest away from the door, but he was in such a deep sleep, he didn't even budge and had no knowledge of whatever this was sneaking into the room.

Gripping the covers tightly around my chin, I cracked one eye slightly to see what was coming my way. To my surprise and somewhat to my relief, I now knew it wasn't the typical type of boogie man I was envisioning to appear, but yet something I was about to learn was much worse, it my father, C.M.

With a flash light in his hand, he started slowly tip toeing his way over to my side of the bed making sure not to make a sound, not knowing I was already asleep or wide awake. I thought maybe he was walking over to his night stand because he may have needed to put something away or needed something inside of it, so I pretended to be asleep.

A few minutes rolled by and I couldn't hear his footsteps anymore, nor did I see the beam from his flashlight. "Good he is gone" I remember telling myself when suddenly I felt a tug at my blanket down by my knees. My heart started pounding, not knowing what was going on and then a faint beam of light that C.M. was holding creeped up under my blanket.

I felt his cold, rough hands feeling his way up my thighs and then grab a hold to the elastic waist band to my pink, polka dotted panties and slowly stated pulling my panties down. I quickly flipped over to my stomach and yanked on the cover little, figuring this gesture would scare him enough to make him think I was waking up and would flee.

It indeed startled him for a brief moment, but he gently flipped my body back over, and like a rabbit dog he was right back on me, to continue.

The cover was slowly raised off of me and he eased himself over the lower half of my body and continued to lower my panties to my ankles. I then felt a cold, wet sensation sliding across the top of my vagina. Next came his fingers tips widely, pulling apart the lips of my vagina as he began to perform oral sex on me. I closed my eyes as tight as I could, praying that he would stop; too scared to scream out to my brother for help. I feared if he knew I was awake, he would beat me or even worse, kill me, so I laid there silent and motionless.

Once, I guess, he satisfied his sick oral fixation, he stood next to the bed staring at me, with my panties still down around my ankles and inner thighs and vagina soaked with his spit. After he stood admiring what he was doing, I heard his footsteps make their way towards the head of the bed, where I was. I closed my eyes back so tight I could see stars in the back of my eye lids. For another brief second there was a silent pause, followed by something that sounded like – ZIIIIIIIIIP- resembling pant zipper being slid down. I barely cracked one of my eyes to see what he was going to do next when a black shadow figure appeared standing directly in front of my face as I laid there. I couldn't recognize exactly what it was in the dark, but suddenly felt a clammy, flesh like object rub across my lips. Again and again I felt this object being rubbed across my lips until it was roughly thrust inside of my mouth 2 or 3 times. He pushed this object so far into my mouth that I was about to throw up and the salt taste that followed was stuck in the back of my throat. Uncontrollably, I started coughing and gagging trying to fight the urge to throw up with tears running down my face. I suppose C.M. noticed that my violent coughing and ridged movements started waking my brother up because without warning, he jumped up and quickly bolted out of the room, slamming the door behind him.

Stunned and confused, I didn't shut my eyes for the rest of the night wishing for the sun to hurry and appear through the blinds to offer some type of securely, but it seemed to take an eternity for that to happen.

    I never thought I would be so happy to hear the sound of a door bell in my life! Without even changing out of my night gown, I ran down the stairs right out of the door, past C.M. without looking back.

    Once secured in the car and out of ear shot of C.M., I started to tell my mother of what transpired that night. Before I had a chance to open my mouth, C.M. flagged us down, before driving away just to lean into the car window and tell her that he checked on me while I was sleeping that night and "the Sand Man had me a headlock", and then walked away.

    Was that his way of saving his own ass just in case I was to tell what happened?

I had no clue who the hell Sand Man was and even more confused that he choose the words "checked on me". That did not deter me because I after he walked away, I described detail by sickening detail right there in the car.

    Tears started to well in the corner of my mother's eyes and her lip started to tremble. She was displaying the type of pathetic look someone would give when they heard those exact details from someone else and didn't want to believe it. Not knowing at this time, my oldest sister had already taken the same steps to tell my mother of what C.M. had done to her years before.

There were no words spoken as we pulled away from C.M'S house after revealing the love of her life was a pedophile and rapist. And as usual, all she did was sit silently and cry. This time was different though; there was no ice cream offering to try and make me feel better. She didn't try to console me, no apologies, hugs or affection as if she blamed me for the disgusting incest acts that he committed.

Since my mother didn't make a big deal about what had happened, I believed that maybe this was something fathers normally do to their daughters, "check them" while they are sleeping. I felt in my heart that something was seriously wrong with what was done to me, my 6 year old brain was conditioned to ignore those rational feelings.

With this being a new norm in my life, every time my mother forced me to spend the night with C.M., knowing what he was doing to me, I started to expect to be "checked" at night while I was sleeping. I stopped being afraid of the creaking door hinges, footsteps in the dark and the beam from his flashlight, it became a part of the nightly routine at C.M.'s slumber parties. Each time, he would add new things to do and other body parts to explore and all I could do is just lay there and take it without complaining.

But finally there appeared a light at the end of the tunnel, after years of nightly checks, the Lord sent in a miracle to save me.

One of C.M.'s other kids, from another one of this side pieces, was coming to Houston from his home town of Connecticut, to live with him due to her mother being terminally ill and in hospice care. Not seeing this miracle as another person's curse, there was finally someone else for C.M. to focus in on to conduct his night checks, instead of me.

The first night of my half-sister's arrival, I was made to spend the night with her at C.M.'s house so she could get adjusted to her new environment a little easier. Now he has his pick of 2 young daughters to choose from, but surely was hoping he would choose her.

Soon after bedtime, like clockwork, the beam of the flash light appeared through the crack of the bedroom door as he choose which one of us was going to be his victim for the night. C.M. decided to give me one last "check" before he started in on his new target with the nights to come because there he was, inching his way towards the twin bed I was sleeping in.

The following morning I woke up to my half-sister sitting on the edge of my bed staring at me with tears in her eyes, with a hint of terror and disgust. "Did Dad check you last night"? I didn't know how else to ask. "No!, I tucked my covers in real tight so he couldn't do what he was doing to you, to me" she replied with a shaky voice.

Many years later, my half-sister and I spoke about the incident and we both agreed that we both carried the feeling of guilt in our hearts for so long because each night we would pray that he would check the other so we could be spared from a night of feeling gross, covered in spit and genital sweat.

Now that my half- sister was settled in, I unapologetically used her as a scapegoat for my reason not to have to go back to spend the night at C.M.'s house. Since the sexual abuse alone wasn't enough for my mother to protect me, I would treat my half-sister like shit and intentionally start altercations just to prove to my mother that we didn't get along. I presented this as a reason why I should stay away from her, so we wouldn't fight and anger the beast. To my surprise this ploy worked perfectly and I was no longer forced to frequent C.M.'s house, even though my mother, knowing he was raping me, would persist to visit C.M. for sexual encounters at night. This wasn't a factor to me because I was finally able to escape his grips and avoided him at all cost, leaving my half-sister there, all alone, in the devil's lair to fend for herself.

Many psychiatrists argue the fact that childhood experiences are what mold our young minds as we develop through life and we were most definitely no exception.

Suffering from such extreme abuse at such a young age, transformed me into an emotionless, insecure vessel of depression before I reached double digits. Going from an innocent child to a developing grown woman mentality, basically overnight has its effects on a child. I turned out to be one most wicket, temperamental, kids on the block.

I would get into fights daily with kids in the neighborhood and even had plans to run away. Whomever, child or adult that did something to piss me off would get the worse of my reactions; I was very explosive and unable to control my emotions.

With being new to Houston, and having no family or friends to turn to, my half-sister received the brunt of my anger. When C.M. went out of town to work for the Houston Rockets, it was arranged for her to come and stay at my mother's house, with my siblings and me, while he was away. She went from one house of abuse with C.M. just to have to come into another house full of people that acted as if we hated her.

My siblings and I would do whatever it took to break her down in tears just because we could. Anything from throwing things at her, not allowing her to eat or use the restroom when she needed to, we found creative ways to torture her.

We went too far one night, when my mother went out with friends and it was just us kids at the house.

We allowed our half-sister to run the water and get into the shower and as soon as she started to bathe and get soapy, we rushed in, grabbed her by the wrist and ankles while she was kicking and fighting, butt ass naked and attempted to drag her outside in front yard, in front of bystanders and attempted to lock the door. She fought tooth and nail, clawing at the wall and grabbing on to anything she could hold onto: the stair rails, door frames and chairs, as we smashed her fingers to let go, so we would be able to expose her naked body to the entire neighborhood. Luckily our little evil asses ran out of energy, dropped her body in the foyer by the front door and aborted the mission with her frantically crying and pleading for us to stop. The second she spotted her moment, she pushed us off of her, jumped up and darted into bathroom, locked the door and refused to come out until my mother made it home.

She tried to snitch when my mother made it home, but we lied and told a totally different story to what had actually happened and was confident our mother would believe us over her; which she did and we totally got away with it with and had to remorse.

What would make kids so devilish towards someone that didn't deserve any of it and was also a victim? There was no denying...we were really fucked up in the head.

Sadly, the craziness didn't cease at harassment and torturing innocent souls. Things started to spin out of control and the treachery drastically escalated in all areas of my life.

I was told on multiple occasions that I had multiple personalities, an anxiety disorder with a touch of ADHD. Most of those personalities were mean, violent and disruptive, while still in elementary school, a brand new personality had emerged; a very sexual personality.

I would provoke and entice the little boys in my class put their hands downs my pants or to touch on the little bumps I called breast. I didn't think much of it or that I was doing anything wrong because I was already used to being touched that way, so I figured that was what I was supposed to let little boys do. My sexual behavior had gotten so reckless, I got my first French kiss and was fingered for the first time by someone other than C.M., in the 3rd grade, at recess on the playground by a classmate and didn't give a damn if we got caught.
With this new thrill, started a very sexually driven, self-destructive path.

I snuck the little boys from the neighborhood into my backyard to play touchy feely and dry hump up against the side of my house or sneak into their bedroom window.

When I was a little older, I met random guys from AOL, the first online chat room, for a quick sexual encounter before I went to school or after the school bus dropped me off and then would never see me again. I would volunteer my body to be these guy's sex toy; guys as old as 50 years old drooling over me. I was wanted! This feeling of being wanted is what eventually got me addicted to giving myself sexually; strictly for that purpose.

Being wild and out of control was extremely easy for a kid that was caught off guard with their parental supervision being eliminated all at once, unexpectedly. This freedom, came with a huge cost.
A freedom that forced me to go from 10 years old to a grown ass woman overnight.

Arriving home from school, after basketball practice, with the house completely empty was a familiar routine during the weekdays. With my sister having extracurricular activities after school and my brother's athletic events, I was normally the first person to make it home at night, for a few hours. I would come in change clothes, raid the refrigerator for snacks and await the arrival of my family to wrap up the night.

Tired from the long day, with my hand in a chip bag, I dozed off watching T.V.
Being startling from the loud noise, I jumped up when I heard the house phone ringing. I took a look at the clock and realized that more than 3 hours passed and no one made it home yet. Usually, if someone was going to be late coming home, it was a rule that we had to call and let someone know; so I naturally assumed that this was that phone call.
But as soon as I answered the phone and heard the panic in my oldest sister's voice, I knew right away, it wasn't the phone call I was expecting.

Not being able to comprehend exactly what was being said, but the tone and the volume of her voice sent me into shear panic mode. "SOMETHING BAD HAPPENED!! OH MY GOD, SOMETHING BAD HAPPENED"!! is all that she could manage to mutter as she started hyperventilating and then the dial tone. Frantic, I tried calling any and every one I could think of trying to find out what was going on? No one knew anything and my mother, brother and 2nd older sister wouldn't answer their phones.
So many horrible thoughts running through my head, my anxiety kicked in and I couldn't catch my breath.

Huffing and puffing while pacing up and down the drive way having a conversation with myself, an unknown car whipped into the driveway like lighting. 'GET IN!! HURRY GET IN"!! My oldest sister screamed at me from the top of her lungs. Not even having enough time to lock the front door, I ran to the car door and jumped in the back seat.

Speeding down road at 100 mph, by passing all stop signs and red lights without so much as tapping the on brakes; I was holding on for dear life. All passengers were deathly silent and none of my questions were being answered. "What the hell is going on?", "What happened?" I demanded answers.

Before anyone even opened their mouths to speak, we were pulling into the ER of Houston Memorial Herman Hospital. Leaving the car parked and running in the front of the building, the tow zone, we all jumped out sprinted through the double sliding doors to find the registration desk. Thankfully we didn't have to wait in a line because once we arrived, familiar faces flagged us down from the end of the hospital hallway, gesturing for us to hurry. In a full sprint, we rushed down to the elevators where we were escorted to the 5th floor, ICU.

Still not knowing who had been injured and brought in, as the nurses and doctors exited a small dark space in the far corner of the Unit with clip boards in hand, we didn't bother to stop and ask any questions.
My mind was racing was we inched closer and closer to the drawn curtain and the person laying behind it.

The conversation in my head was rampant, wondering; was my brother injured during his game? Was my 2nd older sister behind that curtain?...

I braced myself as my oldest sister positioned her hand on the middle of the curtain to pull it back. As the curtain flew back, I stood frozen, staring blankly into the dimly lit space, feeling a numb, tingling sensation all over my body.

My mother was lying there lifeless, half her head shaved bald with tubes and probes connected to her skull. Wires were cascading down her throat through her mouth and stuck to her chest with a monitor attached. The loud beeping and hissing that amplified through my ears was coming from a respirator machine that was breathing for her and keeping her alive. She was on life support barely hanging on.

Doctors, Surgeons and Specialist, going back and forth injecting medicines, changing the I.V. bags and checking vitals, the chaos was non-stop and on-going every few minutes. My sisters left me alone to locate a doctor to find out the specifics of what happened to our mother.

In-between the rush, I was given an opportunity to have a private moment with her. "Mommy...Mommy wake up". There were so many

machines hooked to her, she could have been mistaken for a science experience. No matter how many times I begged her to wake up, she just laid there, in a coma, with that hissing in the background annoying the shit out of me.
The reality of the situation didn't really sink in right away; I was trying to wrap my mind around it. By time I started to grasp the seriousness of the current event, news spread fast and everyone started to arrive at the hospital to learn the status of my mother's condition and how she ended up fighting for her life. There were no shortage of tears as my grandparents were amongst the first to arrive, followed by her friends and colleagues.
On everyone's mind, rest the same question, "What happened"? Since my grandfather was now present, we knew he were certainly going to get some answers.

The conversation between the doctor and my grandfather had come to an end and the only piece of information we were given was that she had been in a car accident that caused detrimental, internal injuries and she wasn't expected to live through the night without assistance. At this horrible moment is when we were instructed to decide whether or not to take her off of life support.

Heartbroken and devastated, my grandmother immediately made that decision without hesitation. "Keep on as long as you can, PLEASE". My grief stricken grandmother was praying for some type of miracle to save her only daughter and was determined to keep that machine breathing for her until her lungs took back over. For hours my grandmother would traveled back and forth, with no less than 50 trips from my mother's room to the chapel of the hospital praying for that miracle.

When we thought things couldn't get any worse than watching our mother lay in this bed dying, the devil himself appeared in the doorway of the ICU...it was C.M.
"Oh Shit"! "Here we go"!...not knowing what to expect from this bipolar asshole, we braced ourselves and prepared for the unexpected.

My sister leaned over and whispered, "Who the fuck called him"? C.M. was supposed to be far away from us, out of town with the

Rockets at a game. How did he find out so fast and fly back to Houston only a few hours from when the ambulance first arrived with my mother? My grandparents announced to us that they found that very suspicious and started asking him some very necessary questions about his knowledge of the accident. A good thing their curiosity hit its peak because right then they received a phone call from one of their good friends and Houston Rocket fan, that delivered some very interesting information.

So happens, way before the doctor even announced my mother's condition status and test results were still being evaluated not knowing what caused her injuries, C.M. went on national television, during the Houston Rocket basketball game and made an announcement that "his wife" had been killed in a terrible car accident and he must leave immediately and will be absent for the remainder of the game.

My mother wasn't dead! She was still fighting for her life when made such an announcement for the nation to hear.

While at the hospital, we already knew he was going to put on some theatrics, drawing attention to himself to gain sympathy from the fans that spotted him at the hospital. He put on an elaborate act in front of the staff, as if he was so hurt and crushed, yet not once did he try to console us kids, as we sat in the same waiting room watching the 'C.M. Show' and waiting to hear word of our mother's fate.

After hours of waiting, the time came when a lone doctor, face hanging towards the floor, slowly entered our waiting area. We all stood at attention, hanging onto every breath the doctor took. In a deep, dragging voice, "I'm so sorry, the swelling on her brain is too severe from her broken neck, and there is nothing that we can do beyond this point". "You should take off her off of Life Support".

"NOOOOOO....NOOOOO", "PLEASE JUST GIVE HER A LITTLE MORE TIME"!! My grandmother was positive with a more time, my mother would recover. "JUST MORE TIME, PLEASE"! She agreed to make the arrangements to pay for all of the extra cost for the extra care. She was willing to empty out their bank account in exchange for my mother's life.

Bizarrely enough, to everyone's surprise, in raged, C.M. leaped up out of his chair and yelled, "She is fucking dead", "Let her go". He kicks his chair across the room and demands to speak to the head doctor immediately.

A few minutes after C.M. pulled the doctor into the hallway, I hear screeching wails coming from the hallway right outside of our waiting room.
Obviously, the doctors were convinced that it was in everyone's best interest to disconnect the life support and let allow my mother to take her last breathes.

How was he able to make this life or death decision? My grandparents fought and argued with the doctors stating that only the next of kin could make those decisions; being that C.M. and my mother were never married, their wishes had sonority. The doctors illegally ignored these facts, and within the next half hour, life support was shut off via C.M.'s instructions. And just like that, with a few digressing beeps and hissing from the respirator, she flat lines... my mother was dead.

The story behind my mother's death was very odd. We hadn't found out the details in its entirety of the accident until we were given the police report a few days after her death. Enclosed within the report were a few statements from people that witnessed my mother's fatal accident, the same individuals that would civilly sue us in the months to come, due to their children being traumatized from watching my mother get killed.

Nonetheless, all lawsuits were thrown out of court, but being a blessing in disguise, these lawsuits enabled every single detail to be laid out on the table for my family to dissect of that dreadful day.

The reports told the story, during the intermission of my brother's basketball game, my mother left the gym making her way to the corner store to buy a Gatorade and never made it back to the game.

She was making a center lane turn out of the gas station on one of the busiest streets in Houston, blindsided, a pickup truck smashed the passenger side door of her little red, Jeep Wrangler. Jeep Wranglers at that time were very weak and flimsy. Plastic windows and paper thin metal for the doors, so I wasn't surprised when I learned that her unconscious body was ejected from the Jeep on impact into 6 lanes of oncoming traffic.

Miraculously enough, all vehicles within striking distance, managed to swerve and avoid hitting her unconscious, body lying in the middle of the highway. Her life would have been spared with the initial impact, but somehow, the truck that slammed into her passenger side, was put into reverse and then spun around to the driver side of the Jeep and ran completely over her, right before parking the back tires on her upper body. This instantly broke her neck and sternum in addition to snapping her spinal cord in half and cracking her skull open, he left my mother with no chance of survival.

As anyone could imagine the next week after my mother's death was a huge blur. So many people stopped by our house to offer their condolences with cakes, pies and casseroles and empty promises to help out in any way they could.

I laid in my mother's bed for days, refusing to get up, drowning in my tears. I went without food and water for days not wanting to move because I was afraid that if I did I would lose my mother's scent that was on her sheets and pillows.

Along with the pain of losing my mother, I was now stuck with the paralyzing thought of who was going to take care of me now that she gone. I was now completely defenseless against the most terrifying person in my life.

Being in a daze after her death, I barely noticed his presence anytime C.M. would come around. One thing I did recognize was C.M. was surely finding himself spending personal time over my mother's house more frequently after her death. Majority of the time, he would only come by when my siblings or I were away from the house. He would use the spare key he made, enter our house and rummage through all of my mother's belongings as if he was desperately searching for something. We would return home and all of my mother's jewelry and documents such as the house deed, insurance papers and anything else of importance missing; all other irrelevant documents and items were thrown about her bedroom like a hurricane touched down.

One early morning, C.M. show up at the front door of our mother's house, realizing his spare key didn't work anymore, he started banging on the door, furiously like he was the Police. BANG... BANG...BANG.. "Open the Mutha Fucking Door Now"!!, he recited over and over as loud as he could until we unlocked the door allowing him in; in the process waking up the nosey ass neighbors to where they came out there house in their robes, standing on the sidewalk watching. My 2nd older sister, with no fear, opened the door and just stood there in the doorway, refusing to allow him to enter. He shoved the door open and muscled his way into the foyer. Without so much of a good morning from his crusty ass lips before he aggressively demanded for my sister to fetch my mother's jewelry box. He claimed that every piece of jewelry my mother processed, he purchased and he wanted all of it back. Without thinking twice, my sister yelled back at him, "Hell No"! We knew she just signed her death warrant with this gesture and considered that to be a suicide mission. "What the fuck did you just say to me?" Before he ended his sentence, C.M. wrapped his hands around my sister's throat and tried to squeeze the life out of her. Her face was turning bright red and her eyes were about to pop out of the sockets. Trying her hardest to catch her breath, she hit him with a swift elbow to the bridge of his wide nose to loosen his grip. Two more elbows came flying towards his face fast and hard, to where he had no choice but to release her. "I will fucking kill you, you bitch"!, C.M. professed as he geared up to charge at my sister and attack once again.

Preparing to pounce, having intentions to seriously hurt my sister, at that exact moment, a 6'1, 250 lb. veteran steps through the front door with my grandmother trailing close behind him. Even though my grandfather's appearance was the most intimidating out of the pair, my grandmother was the one with the biggest bite; she was the first one to confront C.M. "If you touch these kids again, I will lynch your ass like they should have when it was legal". My father's anger was quickly redirected from my sister to my grandmother, as he took step forward giving the impression he was about to hit her. My grandfather took a giant step in front of my grandmother, looked down on this shrimp of a man and in a low tone said, "I Dare You", standing there ready for combat.

We could tell this caught C.M. by surprise due to him previously sending my grandparents' death threats in the past, threatening to burn their house down on numerous occasions with no recourse; I have never seen so much fear in a man's eyes, then what I had just witnessed. C.M. took a few steps back and bolted towards the front door to exit. "You take care of these bastards then"! and vanished as quickly as he appeared.

After the confrontation, things were eerily quiet for a day or so, I guess because the primary focus now was arranging my mother's funeral that was supposed to take place within a weeks' time. Naturally, my grandparents wanted to make the burial arrangements to give their only baby girl a proper burial. Seeking revenge for the humiliating defeat he had just suffered, he made a public announcement that he had already began to organize a Grand Funeral for my mother's home coming.
Not wanting to cause any further commotion or a public scene, they had no choice but to sit back and allow for things to unfold. Hardly being able to stomach to fact that he was making the arrangements, my grandmother already knew that allowing C.M. have authority to control the services was a mistake.

The day was drawing near to put my mother to rest and there was no word about how the funeral arrangements were proceeding. C.M. wouldn't give them any information and continued to be a dick about allowing my grandparents to help.
So three days before the ceremony was to take place, my grandmother took it upon herself to call the funeral home just to make sure her daughters funeral was going to be what she felt my daughter deserved. The angels must have sent my grandmother a sign to give her the notion to call because the mortuary was just hours away from cancelling my mother's funeral due to C.M. paying to the Director with a bad check that bounced and then he refused to answer or return any of the funeral home's telephone calls.

No more than 2 hours after that informative phone call, my

grandparents made their way to Houston with an $8,500 check in hand and paid the balance in full so the Home Going Ceremony would commence as scheduled.

Before leaving the funeral home, my grandparents made it their business to retrieve a copy of the bounced check C.M. used to pay with, for their own records, and still have that very copy today, 20+ years later.

It wasn't such a shock that C.M. actually wrote a bad check for my mother's funeral; that fact of the matter is he wrote bad checks ALL THE TIME! At the grocery stores, our school's cafeteria for our lunches, gas stations, restaurants... EVERYWHERE...on a regular basis!! Within a month's time, he would literally distribute hundreds of bad checks.
It came to the point where his name was put out on the hot check list and establishments refused to accept any other forms of payment from him, besides cash.

Any normal citizen with even one bad check that wasn't cleared would be charged with theft by check and jailed. But Oh No, not C.M., a constable from the area would actually come to his front door just to warn him about a warrant being issued for his arrest. C.M. would basically tell the officer that it was a mistake and he would clear everything up right away. He would the end the conversation with a promise to give the officer Houston Rockets game tickets and that was that; no arrest, just a friendly warning.
The officer casually walked away with a smile on his face, happy to have conversed with a celebrity. No courts date, repercussions or punishments, C.M. seemed to be above the law.

Now that the funeral was back on schedule, we had to continue to prepare for the dreadful day that lied ahead of us. We still had to task of going shopping to find a nice outfit for my mother to wear in the casket. Since I was the baby of the family, everyone decided I should be the one to pick out what our mother should be buried in. I didn't think it was a privilege at all for a 10 year old to have to pick out a "dirt shirt"; it was cruel to me, but I had no choice.

The day that would change our lives forever had finally arrived and it was time for us to go and say our final goodbyes.

We pulled up to the funeral home and you would think it was Elvis Presley's funeral because there was hundreds of people lined up outside waiting to enter the building. Channel 11 and 13 News were camped outside along with the others, with their cameras and reporters ready with questions. Our limo drove around to the back of the mortuary to avoid the curious audience, most at which didn't even know my mother, but just wanted to view C.M.'s dead mistress.

Once we made it inside, the circus continued. The place was overly crowded from front to back with people I have never seen before. There was even a roped off, VIP section designated for former and current Rockets basketball players to have a viewing section for themselves.

My sisters, brother, grandparents and I began to walk down the aisle together to view my mother's stiff, lifeless body lying there as if she was Sleeping Beauty waiting for her Prince's kiss to wake up. It was a surreal moment; I just stood there starring at her.

Her face was bloated but stiff and hard. Her nose was boney and her skin was a pale grey, a disgusting death color. She didn't even look like my mommy; she looked like a totally different person I didn't know. We took our seats in the front reserved pew and waited for the rest of the crowd to view her body and take their seats. With hundreds of people present, the viewing was non-stop, person after person walking up to her casket and then over to us to give words of encouragement for our grief. I wasn't really listening to a word anyone was saying and barely made eye contact with anyone.

As the last group of people started walking towards the casket, I noticed some unwelcomed faces approaching. I knew my eyes weren't deceiving me when I heard my sister proclaim, "I know good and got damn well this nigga didn't bring these bitches here"! Proudly wobbling their fat asses down the aisle, was my mother's well known enemies, C.M.'s other mistresses, displaying the ultimate form of disrespect.

After they walked up to her casket, they turned towards the front pew where we were seated and had the biggest smiles on their faces, showing satisfaction from what they just saw. The Ushers and individuals that were seated closed to us had to run to our seats, grab us and calm the family down because there was about to be bloodshed and weave slung. Luckily, the director escorted those women out of the building, knowing there would be a few more funeral arrangements taking place if they didn't leave quickly.

C.M. was in the front pew on the other side of the church watching like he had no clue who those women were. I'm sure he had that gut feeling to stay far away from us while he was putting on his Academy Award winning performance of the distraught spouse besides himself from her death. He resembled a character from a movie that would throw themselves on the coffin and scream, "Take me Lord, Not Her, Take me Lord"! He had the tears rolling down, booger and snot bubbling out of his nose with shaking and convulsing; it was definitely a hilarious, but a ridiculous episode to witness.

The most riveting hour of the funeral, what I will never be able to forget is when we discovered that the man that killed my mother was present at the funeral. From the outside looking in, everyone thought that he was there to pay his respects to the woman's life he ended, but why was he sitting right next to C.M. in the front pew? And why did they look so familiar and friendly with each other? To our bewilderment, we learned the man that took our mother's life was one of C.M.'s closest friends. What are the odds??
No one put two and two together? Or did the authorities just overlook this fact and let murder slide through their radar? Even though this may be in the realm of a conspiracy theory without pure evidence to back us up, but not having at least an investigation into the specifics of her accident disturbs my core, still now, many years later.

The funeral was gearing to an end and was time for the burial and final thoughts and prayers at the cemetery. Nowhere near as many people that were at the funeral home showed up at the cemetery once their curiosity was satisfied. None of C.M.'s other mistresses showed up, knowing that we were now in a wide open space, so no one would be able to stop the beat down that they were begging for by showing their faces.

After my mother was lowered into the ground and we received our millionth hug, I was ready to go home, but of course that wasn't possible because C.M. demanded that we were to come to his house for a burial reception, to meet and greet my mother's friends and many colleagues. When we arrived to his house, there was only his friends and women dancing, eating and having a merry old time. Not one person was there to meet and greet us, but just to party with him. If a stranger walked in off of the streets, they would figure it was a birthday party or New Year's Eve, how everyone was laughing and enjoying the evening. We were the only ones there that was feeling sadness and grief which made the pain and grief worse. No one cared how we were doing or feeling, they just wanted free food, drinks and time with a celebrity and I was stuck there watching it.

We tried to go on with life the best that we knew how. Now that my mother was gone, we had to deal with the monster more. Even though, my heart and spirit were filled with grief and I missed my mother dearly, I hung on to the comfort of having my brother and sisters there with me. True, we didn't always get along with each other, but I was certain they would always be there for me. Especially now, to protect me; their young, baby sister from our demon. But just like everything else in my life, I was devastatingly wrong and my life was about to take a much worse turn for the worse than I ever expected.

Unsure if they were tired and fed up with dealing with me or they just didn't love me, but the next time C.M. showed up at our mother's house after the funeral commanding us to pack our shit and to leave the house because it was now up for sale, is when they threw me to the wolves.

Standing firm behind not following a single word C.M. ordered, my brother and sister simply told him "No". They figured, what could he do? The house was in my mother's name and they were never married, so we felt that we had the right to live in the house that we were living in with our mom. There was nothing, legally, he could do at this point to evict us from a home that's not his, so he created another maneuver he was sure would make my brother and sister throw in the towel and vacate the premises.

Since I was a minor and he was on my birth certificate as my father, he turned to me and said, "Go pack your shit, your leaving with me". Thinking I was going to be protected by my brother and sister, I told him "No", just as they had done. Just as the word left my lips, he threatened to call the Police and CPS to come and pick me up and arrest my siblings for kidnapping. Terrified, I looked at my bother for protection and guidance and just like that, with a blank expression on their faces, told me to go and pack my things and to leave with C.M. They literally just threw me away and let Satan have me. They put up more of a fight for my mother's jewelry than they did to keep me.

I believe at that moment, maybe because of shock or just mental shut down, every single emotion, good and bad, in my body had vanished. That day, I lost something inside of me... an experience a 10 year old little girl should never know. I lost the will and desire to live- followed by my first unsuccessful attempt to commit suicide.

Dead to the world mentally, the only thing that kept me alive was my heartbeat.
Weeks had passed and I was now living with C.M. and being forced to return to school because I'd already missed about 15 days of the semester. One of the very last things I wanted to think about was returning to school. I would have to truly face my reality and cope with the traumatic events that just took place; which I didn't want to do, but I would go anywhere just to have time away from C.M.

The last time my classmates had seen or talked to me was when I left school an energetic, funny kid, but now I would be returning as a totally different person; a ticking time bomb ready to explode. This internal bomb was filled with anger, rage, resentment, grief, betrayal and loneliness and the fuse was getting shorter and shorter rapidly. All of my participation in anything came to a halt. I quit doing my school work, sports and all leisure activities I used to enjoy were now nonexistence. I started failing in school with nothing but F's on my report card and would brutally fight anyone, boy or girl for no apparent reason. Even an altercation with one of my teachers erupted when I felt she stepped across me the wrong way which resulted in me being detain and hauled off the Juvenile in handcuffs.

Sitting in the back of the class, I admit I wasn't doing a damn thing. I refused to read the chapters, complete worksheets or anything else I was asked to do. I simply had my hoodie over my head, arms crossed, silent at my desk. "Take the hoodie off of your head and get to work", the teacher raised her voice to tell me. Totally ignoring her words, I continue to sit at my desk silent, refusing to do anything else.

My teacher's despised this new despicable student that showed back up in the classroom and I was determine to make their hate for me grew exponentially. This particular teacher must have been at her boiling point with me when she stood at the head of the class and told me, "Maybe if your mother would have taught you some manners before she died, I wouldn't have to put up with you". Before I could calm myself down, I leaped out of my desk, picked it up with both hands and chunked it across the room to where she was standing. I was seeing red as the entire class had to grab me and pin me to the wall to keep me from assaulting her. Campus Police officers rushed in a seconds after someone pressed the panic button on the wall, hemmed me up against the lockers, handcuffed me and escorted me to Harris County Juvenile Detention Center in the back of a Fort Bend School District police car where I remained until C.M. decided to come to have me released and persuade the teacher and district not to press charges.

The remaining years of middle school were spent being a terror to teachers and students I didn't like, but thankfully I found ways to tame my anger. Besides fighting, basketball helped me relieve the frustrations I had festering inside of me. I was the best female basketball player in the school and this skill helped my attitude tremendously and improved my grades, due to not being able to participate without passing grades or discipline referrals. Temporarily it seemed as if I was pulling myself back together and getting my sanity back; but like I stated...Temporarily.

Once I entered High School, it was whole new can of worms. Now living with C.M., in one of a high class areas on the outskirts on Houston, I was registered in an uppity, tight ass, rich school. In total, there was maybe 10 black students, including myself, in the entire school. I was determined to keep my act together academically to ensure my position on the basketball team, but the life I was leading outside of school was were the problems arose. No one could tell me anything; I did what I wanted to, when I wanted to without fear of C.M. And to add fuel to the fire while on this dangerous road of rebellion I was determined to stay on, he moved in one of his girlfriend's daughter into his house with me. This girl was just as screwed up in the head as I was. By the age of 15 she had already been rapped, kidnapped and beaten so just imagine the influence she had on me.

Having someone around the same age that I had something in common with, automatically she became my running buddy, especially when it came to guys. She went right along with my decisions without question and we started roaming the streets doing things we had no business doing at our age.

God works in mysterious ways, even though I didn't think so at that time, but my hot twat days were slowed down by my brother and sister having to move in with me at C.M.'s house because somehow he was able to transfer my mother's house into his name, without so much as going through probate, and sold her house right from under us.
I had no choice but to stop my late night rendezvous' with my new house mate because even though I was still pissed off at them for abandoning me, I was trying to hide this wild side that my siblings have never seen before and never wanted them to see.

It was nice to have my brother and sister around again I guess; it didn't feel as lonely anymore. I didn't feel as if I needed their protection from C.M. any longer; he hadn't tried anything sexual for quite some time. I assumed I was too old and he was uninterested in me now and I am sure he knew I wasn't going to accept the beatings without a fight, so he pretty much left me alone.

Although the sexual and physical abuse had stopped, the verbal and mental abuse continued. As you already noticed, C.M. was a classic, narcissistic womanizer, but what's strange is he always went after the morbidly obese, unattractive women. All of these woman were no less than 350 lbs., no exaggeration; they were huge and smelled like rotting fish or soar milk. Each night he would have a different Hippo come over and would take them up to his private quarters, in the upstairs area of his bedroom for the night.

The most gut wrenching detail about his nightly sex-capades with these gigantic women, was the fact that his private quarters, his game room, although the entrance was all the way on the other side of the house, the walls were conjoined and my room was adjacent to his; we basically shared a wall. Every single one of his sexual encounters would extend into the early hours of the morning regardless if it was a school night or weekend, and all I heard was his Oldie's Collection music playing, accompanied by moans and screams through the way too thin sheet rock.

As if that shit wasn't gross enough, these woman would try to converse with me when visiting, saying they wanted to get to know me. My mean ass would just look at them in their eyes while they talked, roll my eyes without a word being spoke, turn my back in mid-sentence and walk away. C.M. would be infuriated with how I treated his women and would always say "You should be nice to your new mom". "What the fuck"??!!, was all I could think to blurt out when he made those statements. He would look at me with such a grimace gaze as if he was plotting my death, as I feel he did my mother when she crossed him the wrong way, and would tell me aggressively to "Shut the Fuck up and go upstairs".

That very same night, when the first left, only a few hours later, I was greeted yet again by another Elephant that was there to bedazzle C.M., but this particular encounter was different.

Usually I would ignore this lady like all the others, but I immediately noticed that she was wearing something very familiar that I have seen for many years growing up.

Underneath her neon green, sequenced blouse with purple sleeves, looking like a big ass skittle, there was a very shiny stone that sparkled hanging from a sliver chain.

Once noticing this necklace, I ran upstairs to my room, reciting repeatedly, "This motherfucker better not have", checked my supposedly hidden jewelry box and discovered it was gone!!

This bitch was wearing the 2 ct. diamond necklace my mother had given to me before she died. I never noticed that it was missing because since it was supposed to be hidden in my jewelry box, I neglected the check regularly to make sure it was secure.

Once I discovered my necklace was missing, I ran back downstairs with the intentions of ripping my necklace off of her fat ass neck, but by time I made it down they had already vanished behind closed doors. I sat there, right beside his locked room door for hours, waiting for them to emerge from his sex chamber. To my dismay, when she exited the room following behind C.M. hand and hand, the necklace had been removed, but in its place, he had given her my mother's night gown that we bought for her one Mother's Day. Distracted by this sight, the necklace totally slipped my mind as an evil grin appear simultaneously on my face and slowly walked away plotting my revenge.

He went on about his day very content knowing how much I was upset by the situation, but not knowing what my unstable mind was conjuring up.

With hours of just sitting in my room, starring at the wall resembling a psych patient, I finally had a solution to my problem; "I am going to kill him".

Not yet having a plan, I kept my eyes open for every opportunity that presented itself. Brainstorming, I came up with options such as: poisoning his food when one of his women came over to cook for him and I would slip a dosage of rat poison in the sauce, but then again, they rarely left the food unattended, so I figured that plan wouldn't work. I thought up so many different alternatives, but the chance never seemed to present itself in order for me to execute; my patience starting to wear thin and my anger and the pressure was building dramatically. It was dire for me to find an activity to distract my mind from what I was planning so I decided to focus all my energy on basketball once again, the vice that saved me in middle from the same dark thoughts I couldn't shake. Early morning workouts and basketball practices seemed to be helping get my mind back to some sort of an equilibrium.

As the days passed, so did the urges and desires to end it all for C.M. Those evil thoughts were almost, completely vanquished but suddenly returned with a vengeance when C.M. put me in yet another stressful situation that blew my over the edge.

Being on my birth certificate as my father and now our legal guardian, the courts granted him access to collect my brother and my Social Security checks. C.M. receiving our checks wouldn't have been a negative issue if he had intentions on making sure that we were taken care of with the money. I desperately needed an upgrade from the too small middle school clothes and shoes I was still trying to wear. I approached C.M. and requested to use a portion of my Social Security money on new clothes and shoes for the up and coming school year; my request was automatically denied, "There is only enough money to pay bills", he said to me angrily. Knowing there was nothing that I could do, I gave up on the hopes of getting rid of my old torn clothes that I could barely fit.

Until one day, I was ease dropping on a conversation between C.M. and one of his new baby momma's trying to acquire any information I could use against him, when I overheard him planning on giving her the money he was receiving from our checks to use on his new son. My blood was boiling...

I already knew our money wasn't being spent on bills like he wanted us to believe because every single out of state trip he took with the Houston Rockets, the electricity, water or phone would be disconnected for days. When this happened, C.M. didn't give a shit, my brother called him to inform him the water was cut off one time and he literally instructed us to bathe in the neighbor's water hose until he made it back into town, and then refused our calls for the remainder of his trip.

A positive (well not positive because it was illegal) that came from this craziness was that we taught ourselves how to turn the water and electricity back on after the utility company would disconnect them. We became experts at reconnecting the utilities in C.M.'s absence, but then disconnecting them once again before he returned home from his trips; he had no clue. He was satisfied with 'knowing' that we were suffering and all alone having to depend solely on him to survive as he traveled the world.

Although the attempts to end his life were futile, I was once again searching for the perfect time to free myself from this monster's grip and the tremendous amount of hate I harbored for him.

Finally, I found my only chance to carry out this poorly thought out plan to stop C.M. from breathing for good. Here we go.... I'm Ready!!

It was extremely late in the night; one of the rare nights he didn't have a groupie over to play. My brother didn't realize I stole the 22 caliber pistol he had stashed under his mattress for my own personal use. I tip toed down the stairs to the living room, where C.M. would sleep on the floor, in front of the T.V. when he didn't have company.

Slowly, I approached his sleeping body and exposed the gun from behind my back.

KILL HIM!! KILL HIM!! The voices in my head were relentless, as I stood over him pointing the barrel of the 22 caliber directly at his temple. He was still asleep, so I pressed down a little harder trying to wake him up so he could look into my eyes before I ended his miserable life. As he opened his beady, little eyes and tried to focus, it seemed as if time stood completely still for that short moment. I could see every single dust particle floating around the room in slow motion. The scent of his morning breathe resonated throughout the air as he screamed "NO...PLEASE....WAIT!!" and begged for his life.

KILL HIM!! KILL HIM!! The voices were running rampant in my head... KILL HIM!!

All of a sudden a sense of calm washed all over my body as my finger started to pull down on the trigger.... BOOM!!

Is he dead? I kept repeating to myself; hoping he was. Within a few seconds of pulling the trigger, I jumped up, trembling in my bed, drench in a cold sweat. "Fuck!! It was just a dream"... but it felt so real. Just to make sure I wasn't really a murderer, I tip toed down the stairs just as I did in my dream, peeked around the banister and low and behold, there he was alive, still breathing, asleep, on the living room floor in front of the television.

Even though, during the split second I was extremely disappointed, after I woke up and realized I didn't execute my master plan, later on I was actually relieved it was just a dream. Within the next few weeks, I was pleased to notice that C.M. was in the process of doing the job himself. I had that feeling that my days of living with C.M. were numbered.

He started dating girls younger and younger, falling in love with them and losing his damn mind when they broke up with him. The first break down came with this 21 year old Latino girl that used him for money, expensive trips and a car, then left him after she bled him dry because she was pregnant with twins and her husband that was about to be released from prison. This was shocking to me because I thought he was the tin man and didn't have a heart, but obviously that old, rotten thing was broken and caused him to lock himself in his house with a gun and threatening to kill himself. Personally, I was rooting for him to use the gun, but it seemed like out of all the people that rushed over to show him support during his mental episode, I was the only one hoping for the worse. It's sad to say, I must admit, but I found his little insane performance very entertaining and rather amusing.

After hours of talking to him from the windows, his friends convinced him to surrender and check himself into a psychiatric facility for evaluation. He complied and was escorted that night to checked himself into the Coo' Coo's nest.
Unfortunately, he checked himself out the very next morning in fear of his reputation being soiled, but that was one of the only nights my siblings and I were able to relax without sleeping with one eye open or a folding chair lodge up against the door knob. This bliss abruptly ended once we heard his Expedition pulling into the driveway.

A fun tradition my siblings and I had when C.M. was arriving back to the house and we heard the car approaching, we would all try to run up the stairs first, pulling each other back trying to stop each other from taking the lead of making it up the stairs. The last one in the pack running up the stairs was usually spotted by C.M. and called back downstairs for either questioning or scrutiny for departing as fast as we did without greeting him.

It was blatantly obvious that while in the looney bin, he had festering aggression towards me, because he felt as if I was the one that chased her away.
Nooooo.. it couldn't be that she wanted to leave because his soul was dark and he was a disgusting human being that barely washed his ass.... Nope it had to be my fault.

Ok, ok, ok... I might have played a major role in the ultimate decision of this young, pregnant broad leaving him, but what can I say? I didn't like her and she didn't like me and the altercation that transpired between the two of us must have sent chills up her spine and convinced her to flee.

You see, one of the perks of being a celebrity's kid, we tried to take advantage of every chance we could, was that we were invited to many events and different trips. He always wanted to play the wonderful family man and father to the public, so we were required to attend these carefully selected events that were scheduled. I didn't mind too much to travel with him on this next trip coming up because it was going to be a 7 day NBA cruise to the Bahamas and even though C.M. bringing this girlfriend that hated me, my sister and half-sister would be traveling with me so I figured it would be fun.

With the agenda on making my cruise experience an unpleasant one, this broad had an idea to fuck with me and make smart comments and gestures towards me, knowing what my reaction would be, in an attempt to get me punished. Her ultimate plan worked perfectly because I exploded and turned that lady every way but loose. Things between the two of us got so hectic, the animals in the petting zoo we were standing next to on the island the cruise ship was ported on, starting going wild; screaming and banging on their cages.

After I showed my crazy side to her, she ran over to C.M. with balling in tears and by the look in his eyes I could tell I was about to get it in the worse way. For the remainder of the cruise, the only words spoken to me from either one of them was when C.M. told me in a deep, devilish voice. "When we get back [to Houston] you're gone".

I guess my threats to "throw her ass over board", didn't sit too well with her because I noticed it put a damper on their romantic atmosphere during their time spent together for the duration of the trip. This was the beginning of me being known, as single handedly, destroying their blossoming relationship.

    Once we landed back in Houston after the cruise was over, C.M. was eager to show me just how pissed off he was. Before I was able to put my luggage in my room upon arriving back to his house, he was yelling my name to come back downstairs to face his wrath. I took a deep breath and headed towards the stairs. Right before I made it to the top of the stairwell to walk down to face Satan's spawn, I heard 2 voices starting a conversation. The voices were sort of familiar, but I couldn't make them out from where I was positioned. I slowly lowered myself down a few steps and it was clear who was raising their voice, initiating an argument with C.M.; it was my brother. After a few minutes of ease dropping, I gathered that my brother just broke the news of his girlfriend being pregnant. My brother was around 17 years old, a senior in High School and had absolutely no fear in his heart any longer when dealing with C.M. Delighted, this news distracted him from his primary goal he had all week on the cruise because, I, now, the last person on his mind as he battled my brother.

    Not sure why my brother's news was so shocking to him knowing and condoning my bother having sex since he was in the 5th grade, but made him blow a fuse. Maybe it was the mixture of this and the anger towards me, but what happened next thoroughly pleased me, yet was unexpected. I expected, maybe C.M. saying some harsh words, maybe a few threats or furniture being moved, but not this… and not so soon.

    After hearing C.M. excitedly proclaim that we are some, "Ungrateful bastards", and "Some unwanted motherfuckers", he told my brother, "Go upstairs, pack your shit and pack your fat ass sister's shit and get the fuck out of my house"!

    Relieved at what I just heard I didn't even wait for my brother's word to start packing up my belongings, overly eager to get out of there. I was already half way packed before my brother made his way to my room to inform me of C.M.'s decision.

So happy to be escaping Alcatraz and getting away from C.M., his oversized hoes, emotional and verbal abuse, but then had to ask myself, where am I going to go? That was the only question I had. I had no mother, no father and no family because we were stuck in the middle of racial prejudice; the black side despised white people, and my white side despised black people, so we had no one to turn to. All the people that claimed to love us and would do anything for us, turned their backs on us when it came down to showing what they stood for. Just like everyone else, they all stood for materialistic things C.M. provided for them. No matter how wrong he was and always been, no one wanted to help us in fear of losing this celebrity's friendship and the perks that went with it.

My brother and I were trying to come up with a plan before we took the leap back to the streets. Our last resort was to call our grandparents, my mother's folks. Although they displayed a deep disgust for Negros and an even deeper loathe for C.M., they both took the background role and helped us with many things that we needed. We would call them throughout the time we stayed at C.M.'s house to share that the only food available was Lay's Potato Chips, chocolate milk and cookies. Right away they would visit the grocery store and buy items I could hide in my room so I would always have something to eat when I needed.

When my brother and I described what had transpired in lieu of us being homeless, they were more than happy to help get us away from him.

At the last second, when we were leaving C.M.'s house, my brother decided that he was going to live with our 2nd older sister's boyfriend and I was to head out to the country to live with my grandparents.

Now I know I should have been more appreciative of them rescuing me from that hell hole, but as a teenager I couldn't see past my own boobs and didn't want to leave the city and all of the mischief I was leaving behind.

After I showed up at their home, my grandparents quickly took him to court to receive full custody, child support and the social security checks that he was stealing from us.

Once out of C.M.'s house, I started adjusting to my new country life. For the first few months, my grandparents allowed me to reside with my High School basketball coach so I could finish the school year out at my current school without having to transfer to new school so close to the end. But when summer hit, I was a full fledge country girl. I hated it!! We lived in the middle of nowhere. I wasn't allowed outside alone due to the racist families that occupied their neighborhood. I was stuck in the house watching unsolved mysteries and playing dominos with old people. It was in fact quite peaceful, but for a teenage, city girl it was torture. I would go into the bathroom and turn on the bathtub faucet to drown out my tears of dread and despair. My grandparents did everything in their power for me they thought would help. With them, I had a nice home, good food 3 times a day, clean living quarters and washed clothes, and yet, I was horribly depressed; the saddest I have been since my mother died. Maybe it was because I thought of my mom often while I was there. It didn't help that my grandma built a shrine for my mother and I had to look at hundreds of pictures of her on a daily basis and it upset her when I started to cry. I couldn't take it. It was breaking me down mentally. In a fit a sadness, I developed an ingenious plan to run away.

I was going to wait until my grandparents fell asleep, since they went to bed fairly early, I thought this would be the perfect time to sneak out of the window, foot it about 3 miles down the road to the nearest McDonalds and have my boyfriend come to pick me up. I didn't have much planned further than that, but that was a start.

While squeezing my big body through the window, the old window frame must have made too much noise in my attempt to pry it open because as soon as I had one leg outside, me straddling the window seal, I heard my grandfather's footsteps burling down the hall towards my room. I tried to throw my other left over to clear the window, but like most Navy Vets, my grandpa had quick hands. He grabbed my leg so tight, I thought he was drawing blood. I had no other choice but to back track my steps because he wasn't letting go. He look so hurt as he said, "We will talk about this in the morning, now go to bed". Once securely back in bed, he turned on the house alarm, just in case I attempted another escape and he confidently went back to bed. I could hear my grandma muttering trying to figure out what was going on but my grandpa was firm when he said "It is under control". That was her cue to leave it alone and wait for the morning to learn the details.

I don't remember getting any sleep that night, I just looked into the darkness for hours until the first sight of the sun reared its face.

I believe I really hurt my grandparent's hearts with that selfish act because within a month of living with them, they would allow me to move back to the city into an apartment with my oldest sister. They knew it was a terrible mistake to allow this, but being stubborn, I would soon find this out the hard way.

Keep in mind, the sister I was moving in with had much more deeper issues than myself, due to the rape and abuse from C.M. and being a runaway since the age of 13, she had years of street life under her belt with an 8th grade education. She had a few screws loose and wasn't the sharpest tack in the box; a very bad influence over my young, impressionable life.

We moved into a 2 bedroom apartment and transferred to one of the toughest High Schools on the Southwest side of Houston. I was able to blend in and the year started off very well; at school anyway. All the problems that would arise stemmed from me living with my sister and the drama that came with it. The street rat mentality was the only distinctive trait instilled in her. All of the things parents try to keep their kids away from was embedded in this one person and even though she was very pretty with a nice figure, for lack of a better term, she was an alcoholic slob. She never cleaned the apartment, herself and rarely her 3 kids. There would be maggot infested meat packages under the kitchen cabinets and molded bread in the pantry. Roaches and rats moved in and claimed our apartment as their own territory. With the amount of roaches we had, they should have been paying rent. Besides dealing with the pest and rodents that came with the apartment, my sister had another 6'5, 280lb pest I had to deal with.

Without my approval, my sister had a long term boyfriend that was residing with us that would use my sister's face as a punching bag and the kids would witness most of the abuse. Gashes would be ripped into her neck as if he tried to tear her throat out with his bare hands, black eyes were now a part of her normal appearance and the mental abuse he subjected her to never ceased.

One time he left with their newborn daughter and disappeared for weeks, not even calling to let her know the baby was ok. I rarely got involved in their business because no matter how bad he beat her each time, she would always have a reason to take him back. It was like she enjoyed getting pounded on daily or blamed herself sometimes. Just to spare the babies from seeing their mother being attacked, I would take them into my room, blast the music to drown out the fighting screams, followed by the sounds of makeup sex that filled the air. Once I heard this, I knew it was safe to leave the room without the fear of being hit by a flying object, my sister.

I became a heavy pot smoker, a pothead if you will, while living with him and watching my sister get the shit beat out of her every day; pot became my refuge.

Like most things, every bad situation has it day to end. Sometimes they have a happy ending but of course, with our luck, the majority of situation end very badly and this would not be an exception. Things were about to EXPLODE!

Being higher than Sputnik, I got lost on my way home from school one day and arrived home a little later than normal. Approaching my front door, I could hear the kids screaming; a curdling scream that I have never heard from them before which killed my buzz right away. I burst through the door like Kool Aide man and lost it with what I saw.

My sister was raised completely over her boyfriend's head in the air, nearly touching the ceiling and 2 seconds away throwing her across the room. The kids were huddled in a corner, heads buried in each other's arms, helpless. Without blinking an eye, I charged at him like a raging bull. With the glimpse of the attack coming his way, he dropped my sister and braced himself for the impact. Like a chimp, I leaped onto his back and tried to take chunk out of him with my teeth. Being much bigger than I, he had no problem tossing me off of his back and up against the wall where I slid down like a squashed fly. With my adrenaline pumping and the back of my head throbbing from the impact of the hit, I was ready for round 2. By the time I was balanced back on my feet, he was coming at me with arms wide open; that could only mean one thing, he was going to bear hug me. I waited until he was close enough and grabbed the closest object, a table lamp and swung it with all of the power my arm muster up. It was like I was in a horror film, the strike didn't faze him in the least. He caught me with a hard blow to the jaw and I immediately tasted blood. My ears were ringing and I heard something that resembled kids screaming my name. I searched for anything I could get my hands on to knock his head off of his shoulders. But as I reached for my baseball bat lying underneath the couch, my sister yell the most unbelievable words to me. She threatened to call the police on me if I hit him with the bat. Dazed and confused, I thought she was hollering at the man that nearly killed her, but she was actually talking to me.

I was standing there with a knot on the back of my head and a busted lip, trying to save her ass and she threatens to call the cops on me.... Unbelievable!!

Bleeding from my face, I quickly left and decided it was time to find another place to live and fast.

Trying to figure out what my next move would be, I drew up a list of possible places I might be able to go. I knew going back to my grandparents' house wasn't an option and would live in a crack house before I even thought about going back to live with C.M. The only option I had was to call my second oldest sister, the one that abandoned me years earlier, and ask if I could come and live with her and my brother since they just rented an apartment together. I was confident she would say yes because since they betrayed me when my mother died, I figured they at least owed me that much. This sister was already waist deep in her stripping career and had since started using cocaine and alcohol heavily and rarely home, though reluctant to my request, but I gave her a friendly reminder of the heartless bullshit she put me through years earlier. With that, once I jogged her memory, she allowed me to come and move in with her.

Like I said before, my sister was rarely home and my brother was always away chillen with his friends so it was kind of like I had my own place. With the peace that came with it, I started focusing more on schooling and sports rather than guys and finally had no drama to deal with.

That peace only lasted for a few months when we got evicted and had to move in with one of my sister's sugar daddies. It wasn't the Ritz, but at least it was a roof over our heads. I was thrilled that my sister had such wonderful manipulation skills because shortly after we were evicted, my sister finessed her way into the man renting us a townhouse close by my high school.

Now a senior, the remaining time in High School seemed to fly by quickly and it was already nearing the end of the school year. The day for Senior Prom was approaching and I was extremely excited even though I was anti-social and close to 300 lbs., my best friend told me if no one asked me to prom that he would escort me as his date. Thinking I was about to have the best night of my life nothing could bring me down.

Noticeably, the last few weeks before prom, my best friend starting acquiring a new set of friends, 'the modeling crew' of the school that were very popular and started ignoring me. More and more, with each day that passed, he became more distant and stopped talking to me all together.

A few days before prom, it was scheduled for him and I to pick up my dress and shoes from the shop to make sure our colors matched. I called and called but no answer after the 1st, 2nd, 3rd and 4th attempt and he had also missed the last few days of school. I was very concerned about him, not knowing if he was alright because since we became friends, there hadn't been a day that passed that we hadn't talked to or seen each other. Every day at school I searched for him, but he was nowhere to be found and oddly enough he was marked present for each one of his classes.

Prom night arrived and my date was M.I.A. No word from him and I have not seen him in days; I feared the worse. "What happened to him"? my mind kept repeating over and over again. I was in tears thinking he was missing or even worse, dead. I didn't have his parent's number and every time I went by his house, no one would answer the door. He just vanished. I was left sitting at home, in my prom dress with nowhere to go.

The following Monday after prom, I went back to school heart broken and grief stricken thinking my best friend was gone. Trying to get on with my day, I was sitting in the cafeteria admiring everyone's prom pictures since I wasn't able to take any of my own. I was immediately drawn to a set of pictures that I spotted in the back of the stack. The first face I saw was one of the chic's from the 'modeling crew' my best friend recently became a member of and who do you think was standing there in the picture with her, arm and arm, with a big smile on his face? The one and only... My best friend.

My eyes went tunnel vision for a second and all I was able to see was his face. My shock induced daze wore off and tears just started to roll down my face. Betrayal has grown to be an all too familiar emotion I have experienced in life, but this time seemed to hurt just a little bit more.

Thank God I didn't get the privilege of seeing him that day because no telling what I would have said or done to him. I needed a good second to calm down and get a hold of my emotions.

The following week I finally saw him at school again while he was hanging out with his new click and seemed not to have been fazed one bit about what he had done to me. When I walked by him, I didn't speak a word just to see what type of reaction I was going to get out of him. Just like he never knew me, he went about his conversation and refused to even look my way.

One of my defense mechanisms that I had formed over the years towards people that I once cared for, was not dealing with the situation at all and try to push it as far out of my mind as possible. It was just too painful. From that day, I have never talked to or seen him again. Sadly, years later, I found out that he committed suicide.

So close to graduation, I was determined to finish out the rest of the year as a recluse. I refused to interact with anyone and it helped knowing that in a few short months, I would be headed to college, as far away from Houston as possible.

It was 4 long years of stress and drama but I did it; graduating with honors, school was finally over! Preparations for college had already been made, I had a U-Haul truck reserved and my belonging packed ready to leave; I was ready for my new life. I was accepted into each college I applied to: Texas Southern University, Rice University, San Angelo State and Baylor, but I was trying to see Texas in my rear view mirror, so I decided to accept the invitation and Basketball Scholarship to attend Louisiana State University. The only thing in my way now was the 3 months of summer vacation I had to wait out. To make the wait bearable, I applied for summer jobs and was hired at Party City. It felt good finally making a legit pay check and being able to get the things I needed without having to beg some guy for money and or do something I didn't want to do; something strange for some change.

I worked for those 3 months straight, keeping my mind busy, and was able to save a few checks to buy my very own first car, a red 1994 Ford Taurus; a piece of shit, but it was mine. Driving, not having to ride the public Metro Bus anymore was heaven. Having a car enabled my sister and me to be able to do activities we were not able to do otherwise.

My 2nd oldest sister persuaded me to allow her to use my car at night to go to work at the Ice Cream Palace strip club to make more money that we needed. My sister was one of the most popular dancers at this club and come to find out much, much more come.

This sister always got any and everything she desired, from my mother, friends, and every guy that she dated and even from the guys she didn't. I guess that was the incentive that came along with being gorgeous with a perfect body, like she had. She could have been a model if she choose to, but made the horrible choice to dance naked for men and be a video vixen. Her looks were flawless and every man and gay woman wanted her and unfortunately, any man or woman that had money had the opportunity to have her. I tried to mind my own business and show support for anything my siblings decided to do, but when their decisions started to ruin my life and everything I bust my ass for; now, once again, we have a big problem.

It was a normal, mundane night and as usual my sister was preparing for a night of shaking her ass at the Ice Cream Palace. I felt something was off this in particular night. After she took my car keys and departed, I got a horrible feeling in my gut and somehow just knew this night wasn't going to end as it usually had in previous nights.

3 a.m. that morning is when all the chaos abruptly showed its ugly face when the phone started ringing back to back, that early in the morning, I knew something was horribly wrong. I received a phone call from a Bails Bondsman, claiming that the Houston Police Department has a woman in custody. Concerned that it was my sister, I asked the man who exactly was arrested. When he opened the document to read the defendant's name, I thought I must still be asleep because it was impossible for this person he stated to have been arrested; the person was ME! I sat straight up in bed, whipping the boogers out of my eyes and asked him to repeat himself. No matter how many times I asked him to repeat himself, the only thing I heard was my full government name.

Trying to find out why they would be calling ME at home, saying that they have ME in jail, I frantically called around to the different HPD departments to get to the bottom of it.

With those few phone calls, a disturbing conversations with Houston County Jail and the Bails Bondsman revealed that my sister was arrested during a Police raid at her place of employment. My sister along with the other dancers were arrested and charged with prostitution and participating in a Sexual Oriented Business. If my sister was the one that was arrested, why was anyone calling me declaring that I was the one being held in custody?

The truth of the matter was that when my sister was detained, she gave the officers my newly printed paper driver's license, including my personal information from my car's glove compartment and told the cops that she was me to avoid consequences for an arrest warrant she had under her own name.

I was a month away from leaving for college and now my scholarship and funding for school was in jeopardy, not to mention my life, because there was now a prostitution charge on my record.

My car was towed after the arrest, so I had to walk a mile to the bus stop just to take an hour ride Downtown to the HPD county clerk office to get the details of exactly what was put on my record and what I needed to do to file a report for identity theft.

To make sure the correct person was charged, while my sister was still in custody, I gave my finger prints and was issued a Not Me Letter to carry around with me to prove that I was not a prostitute if my background record was ever in question.

The records department of the Houston Court System guaranteed me that the arrest charge would be deleted from my record and transferred to my sister's already lengthy record with using my name as an Alias. Instead of the courts doing what they promised and clearing my record, they did the exact opposite; a huge error was made and they kept the charge on my record and added that I used my sister's name as an alias.

I didn't learn of this error until a month later when I received a certified letter from my college campus threatening to revoke my basketball scholarship and other program initiative I was granted due to my new criminal record. It took weeks to mail in all of the documents acquired to LSU, from the Courts to prove to the University's Dean of Admissions and the Athletic Director that I was not a Hoe and a jail bird, in order to keep my admission acceptance and basketball scholarship.

When my sister was released from jail within the next few days, she tried to avoid coming home for as long as she could knowing what she had coming to her once she walked through our door.

Surely she couldn't stay gone for much longer and I stayed put, waiting for her ass. The jingle of her keys in the door knob woke me up as she tried to sneak in without being noticed. Pitch black with a shimmer of the street lights peeking through the blinds, I watched as the door knob turn slowly while kneeling in the corner, waiting, like a Lion stalking its prey. With her first step inside of the door, I flicked on the lights and like a deer caught in the head lights, she froze stiff. The shock only lasted for a second because before I noticed, she darted up the stairs fleeing to her room before I could grab her. She made it to her room before I could catch up with her and quickly locked the door,

thinking she was safe behind it. I must have thought I was a member of the SWAT team the way I kicked her door off of the hinges and attacked.
Right then, after I whooped her ass, I decided that I was going leave for Louisiana much earlier than planned.
Ecstatic to be leaving the next day, I thought running away and leaving was what I needed to forget and keep all of the bad memories in Houston were they belonged.

    College Bound!! I arrived at my dorm around 2 o'clock that morning and for the first time in life, was able to exhale. Starting a new life away from Houston, those past horrible memories and everyone that helped create them was my motivation to stay on a positive track.

    At first I was dragging ass trying to adjust to this new territory, the people and how slow things where compared to the city; things were much different than life in Houston. In Northern Louisiana, close to the Mississippi-Arkansas border, the racist and rednecks were in abundance. Confederate flags were displayed in almost every store window and residential neighborhood surrounding my campus and dorm. Thankfully, I wasn't on anyone's radar with racial attacks because with my fair complexion, I seemed to fit in perfectly. I even met a nice man and started dating; finally knew what it felt like to have an unforced, genuine smile on my face.

    A couple of months passed and I was doing fantastic; good grades, a good man; I was loving college life so far and seemed to be what I needed to flourish.
But of course, every time things started to look up for me, the sky came crashing down.
When old folks tell you that family will bring you down faster than your enemies, please believe them, it's the TRUTH!

    Some days earlier, my oldest sister just delivered her 4th child, by the same low life that tried to kill her, and calls me crying saying she was living in a homeless shelter, got kicked out and now living on the streets with my nieces and nephew.
Oh Lord, here we go again!!
Even though the last time I spoke to her was when I had a black eye and a fat lip fighting her boyfriend, it wasn't in my heart to leave the

kids out on the streets with nowhere to go because I felt she didn't deserved shit from me; those babies didn't deserve that.
The very next morning, bright and early, my new boyfriend and I drove 400 miles back to Houston, in his 2 door Saturn, in December's freezing rain to pick up my sister and her 4 kids. It was a miracle we got there safely because the weather was dangerous, wreaking havoc on the roads and lanes were barely visible; especially to a man that had cataracts and a stigmatism in his eye.

After picking up the little tribe, the weather subsided, but the trip back was just as uncomfortable as it was on the way there. His little compact car, made for no more than 4 people was packed from front to back with 3 adults and 4 children; not to mention the 10 trash bags full of clothes stuffed on the floor broad, underneath our feet. In store for another 5 hour trip, packed like a clown car, we were headed back to my dormitory apartment in Louisiana.

Not realizing how much I missed those little brats until I saw their faces again, I was glad I decided to have them live with me. Ever since they were born, I took an active role in raising them so now, at least I could protect them from their unstable, drugged induced mother.

For 6 months, they were hiding in my on-campus efficiency apartment. It was tough trying to keep a 7 year old, 5 year old, 3 year old and a new born quite enough to avoid drawing attention to us, but somehow it worked out. At the end of the semester, with the little money I had saved, we started searching for a bigger place to stay, off campus before I had to face University penalties for having unauthorized inhabitants in the dorms.

Only having a few hundred dollars to spend and not knowing the area well, it caught me by surprise when we ended up rented out a house that had rats that were big as dogs that chewed through the walls. On different occasions we would wake up to use the bathroom, lift up the toilet seat to sit down and there would be a dead rat floating in the toilet water. It was awful!! Even worse, we tried to be smart and put rat poison out around the house to gain control of the infestation not knowing that the rats would drop dead in every room of the house. We figured they would eat the poison and maybe die outside or in a designated corner of the house. We couldn't have been more wrong because once the poison was distributed, within hours we had to watch were we placed out feet because without noticing, we would step on dead baby rats that were scattered throughout the halls. Never in a million years would I think this decision would back fire and affect any animal that it wasn't intended for. To our horror, we awoke one morning to find all of our animals lying on the living room floor, dead. Dogs, kittens and the rats, all of them ate the poison; it looked like a suicide cult for pets.

Devastated by the animal's deaths, we tried to look at the positive aspect of the situation; now all of the pest were gone and we could sleep without the fear of a gigantic rat chewing through the walls and falling on your face while in bed.

Besides living in that petting zoo, I started to regret rescuing my sister from being homeless in Houston and sacrificing my University living quarters because she took a drastic turn for the worse. For the first few months of her moving to Louisiana with me, she was decent with no issues to report, that was soon to change. Once comfortable with her new lifestyle, she reverted back to her old ways: sleeping with different men, drinking excessively, using cocaine and severely mistreating her children.

During my first class of the day, at the start of a new school week, I received a call from my nephew's school urging me to come to meet with the Principal immediately. Without explaining to my professors my sudden urgency to leave, I snatched my backpack and sprinted to my car, fearing the worse. Once there, I didn't even bother to find an available parking spot; I pulled up in front of the elementary school, in the loading zone, and hauled ass inside. Before I spotted anyone's face, I noticed this pungent odor coming from the front office. A smell was strong enough to make you gag if you don't hold your nose. I made my way around the clerk's desk to approach the Principal's office holding my breath because of the smell and what I saw next literally brought tears to my eyes.

My 3 year old niece had walked a half a mile to school with my 7 year old nephew, at 6:30 in the morning, by themselves. And would you believe that this wasn't even the worse part of about it; they were wearing clothes 5 sizes too big that were drenched in dog piss with big chunks of dog shit stuck to their shirts. I was mortified yet humiliated with these people thinking I was responsible for the condition these kids were in.

My sister was a CPS case waiting to erupt and I was the only one that could help.

Stressfully, having to study for my full time class schedule, attend basketball practice and then come home and take care of 4 kids and their coke head mamma, proved too much to handle for me. Without her permission, I contacted my grandparents, explained the dire situation the kids were in and organized a time and place for them to come and take 2 of the kids back to the country with them. My sister had no clue what was about to transpire, until she witnessed my grandfather's truck pulling into the driveway. "What the hell are they doing here"? I refused to even waste my breath to explain because when the oldest and the youngest emerged from behind the bedroom door with bags packed of clothes, she went ballistic. "You aren't taking my mother fucking kids"! "Give me my kids"! Very calmly I looked my sister in her eyes and warned her, if she didn't allow those babies to go and have a good life away from her abuse, I would call CPS myself and have charges brought against her for neglect and child abuse.

My sister hurled every curse word and derogatory name she could think of at me, as my grandparents departed with two of my nieces. Now I had to figure out where the other two children were going to go, having no family other than me. I knew my sister was going to put up a fight now that she was sure I was taking all the kids away from her and her government benefits will be revoked. Before I had a chance to make my getaway with my niece and nephew, my sister took them and disappeared.

I wasn't sure if I should call the police or go searching for her, but I knew the kids were in danger. I drove around for hours checking the areas my sister would frequent with no luck. I eventually gave up and realized that all I could do at this point was pray for them and let go. Remembering I wasn't very mentally stable myself, it was time for me to get back to focusing on better myself. I had to learn I couldn't save the world, though I tried.

My prayers had to have worked because shortly after my sister vanished with my niece and nephew, I received yet another disturbing phone call, at 4 a.m., but this time from the Police Department. Already knowing my sister pulled another irresponsible stunt, I anticipated CPS getting involved and putting the kids in foster care. To my surprise I was asked to come down to the station and pick them up and take them with me. I would be given the option to legally care for them without interruption from my sister. Like I always have done, I dropped everything and in an instance and I was speeding down to the station. I was instantly directed to a back office when I cleared the metal detector at the Police Station, where my niece and nephew were fast asleep on a pallet the Detective made for them. "Why are they here"? confused not seeing my sister nowhere in sight. With a sincere, pitiful look in her eyes, she told me that out of 25 years of her on the force, had never seen such a sad case. She had spotted and picked up my niece and nephew from walking on a major freeway by themselves at 1 o'clock that morning. Neither one of them had on shoes and both wearing only night gowns. She had traced where they had been walking from, which lead her to a sky rise apartment building with flames blazing out of windows, fire trucks and ambulance swarming the building. With tears in her eyes, she told me a guardian angel had to be watching out for them because my nephew was the one that started the fire. My sister left them alone in the apartment for an unknown amount of time and my nephew tried make dinner for him and his sister. Being only 7, practically a baby, he accidently ignited a dish rag that was left on the stove. They assumed that once he noticed the fire, he gather his sister and left for safety.

Within the next few weeks, I was granted custody and before being questioned by police, my sister once again vanished.

After being granted custody of the kids, I was more than grateful for my sister's absence from the kids' lives; it was a much better situation for them that way, but as always made things worse for me. Now having to care for two young children, get a job, and being a full time student; there was no possible way I could continue practicing and traveling with the basketball team. I had to miss practices and away games because I was the only person available to care for them. I ultimately had to make the decision to sacrifice everything I have worked so hard to accomplish, relinquish my scholarship and surrender my position on the basketball team. I was devastated, but I knew the lives of these two innocent kids where worth way more.

Things were getting rather difficult for me having to adjust to becoming a mother figure overnight. My grandparents were able to continue life uninterrupted as experienced parents and already 'been there and done that', so I took comfort in listening to my granny's advice regarding handling the kids and what we could do to get my sister's head out of the clouds. She had suffered the worse abuse out of all of the siblings and needed the most help mentally. Going to therapist, counselors and even rehab didn't help. What would help her let go of all her pain and internal misery she was carrying around allowing it to kill her slowly.

One night I was venting to my grandmother about being fed up about how our life has been and how the person that made it that way is living a carefree life with no remorse of what he had done. We all were mentally unstable, had trust issues and choose drugs as a vice to cope with the abuse he subjected us to with no consequences.
She interrupted me with a statement that rocked my soul and put some fire under me. She said that she checked and within the up and coming year that my oldest sister's statute of limitations on the abuse she had endured would be expiring. This means my sister only had a few months to formally inform officials of what C.M. had done her and finally hold him accountable for the extreme abuse he subjected her to.
My first thought was, that was not going to happen. I truly doubted my sister would speak of any of the tortuous experiences she gone through, but one thing I decided; if she was going to go with it, I wouldn't leave her hanging and be right there by her side to tell my story as well. Leary of the idea of pressing charges so we could tell the world what he had done to us, due of the public exposure that it attract, was an overwhelming notion. Where we were in our lives; so

depressed, misguided and lost, were we ready for that?

I contemplated on the idea for a couple of weeks, weighing the pros and cons if we decided to go through with it. I refused to speak to my sister so my grandfather reached out and was able to get in touch with my sister to discuss the possibilities and what it could do to help her let go or the past and start to heal. Just like the rest of us, she was uncertain about that leap and was scared to pursue the charges. Not sure what my grandparents spoke into her ear, but it was the determining factor that gave my sister the courage to agree to open the case and my grandmother already knew who she was going to contact to get the ball rolling.

The first agency that contacted us to start the investigation was the Texas Rangers. This initiated the charges being officially filed and the courts giving permission to proceed with the investigation. The initial charges read as followed: 3 counts of indecency with a child and 2 counts of aggravated sexual assault against a minor. These charges were too weak in my eyes, but ignorant to legal proceedings, I figured it was a start to help best assist with the healing process from the years of silent pain and suffering.

After the charges were filed and the Grand Jury indicted C.M., we stayed glued to the news stations to see what Houston would be saying about the females attacking their beloved celerity.

C.M. made it his mission to appear on T.V. making a spectacle of himself. He would make numerous appearances on local and national news stations broadcast crying and pleading to get his "loving" family back. The funny part about his T.V. speeches; whenever C.M. wanted to create tears to gain sympathy from his adoring fans, he would carry a washcloth with him full of Vicks Vapor Rub to rub across his eyes as if he was wiping tears, in turn make his eyes water as much as needed them to creating the illusion of tears.

It took about a year for the investigation to be completed with the interviewing a slew a people, family, co-workers and basically anyone we dealt with in our lives for information good or bad about us.

During the investigation, we were warned that many surprises may arise as new information was being discovered, so we prepared ourselves for anything, but once again, nothing could prepare for the information that was discovered.

The Texas Ranger that was in charge of our case called a random conference with my sisters and me with something that would blow our case wide open.

When the Ranger interview C.M's other daughters, our half-sisters, regarding the allegations, they also admitted that they were also raped and molested by him. A secret they have been holding in for so many years, when asked, came spilling out in a moment of relief; lifting a burden off of their shoulders.

I thought we were the only victims. I never knew and didn't even think in a million years that it happened to them, but a pedophile won't stop collecting victims and he took advantage of any chance he had, I see, regardless of which daughter it was.

The worse part about the ordeal was the negative comments that the public would openly make. Just because they watched his smiling face, colorful suites and Youth Academy full of a number of little girls for him to choose from, he was supposed to be a standup guy, capable of doing no wrong, but in reality he was one of the most despicable men alive; a monster behind closed doors. According to the consensus of Houston, we were some money hungry bitches that were just trying to ruin his reputation to get all of the property and inheritance that was left behind from my mother's death that he stole from us.
They had no idea that he was actually broke and owed the IRS a lot of money and all of the money he stole from my mother's accounts that was left to us after she died, was already spent.

The madness didn't stop there. Once the trial actually began, many crazy people that we never even met made claims to have known us, or have talked to us before about conspiring against C.M. Different people he hired, like the tattoo artist that gave me my first tattoo at the age of 12, to commit perjury. He was also represented by one of the best lawyers in Houston. The same crooked lawyer that represented all of the sports figures and other celebrities.

After the full year of investigations, while receiving death threats, our cars being tampered with and house broken into, it was my turn to testify. I was flown from Louisiana to Houston to face the monster that was our father. Called to the stand one by one, the interrogation process lasted for 9-13 hours per witness. The lawyers drilled and questioned us about every single detail of our lives. Drilling questions like: "How many boyfriends did I have?, When was the first time you had sex?, How many men have you had sex with?"... on and on. They asked the most embarrassing questions anyone could have asked in front of a crowd full of strangers and we had no choice but to shame ourselves and tell the truth about our juvenile indiscretions from the past. People that didn't know me, now knew every intimate detail about my life. Even things I had kept secret and hidden for so many years were now out in the open for public scrutiny.

Speaking of exposed secrets, during the trial, one the most life changing, diabolical secrets was revealed; a secret that would shift the course of my oldest sister's life forever.

During her hours of ridicule on the stand, the biggest bomb was released in the court. What we found out proved that our mother was even worse than we thought she was. While being questioned my sister was handed a stack of papers and was instructed to read the selected, highlighted passage aloud. What she read stopped her in mid-sentence. As it turns out, when she was born, her REAL father signed over his parental rights; C.M. was not my sister's real father as we were taught to believe. Our mother changed my sister's last name to hide her true identity and this was the cruel way she found out, blindsided by evil lawyer representing an evil man.

The trial revealed many unpleasant things about all of us. All the information and truths that we told, C.M.'s lawyer tried to paint the worse picture possible of us and the type of people we were. According to the picture painted, we were lying, ungrateful, fat, crack head sluts trying to get a quick buck from a man that tried to give us a privileged life. They tried every trick in the book to destroy or character and discredit us, by any means necessary.

Regardless of the refusal to request a change a venue motion, I was pretty confident that he was going to be put under the jail for what he had done to us because while testifying, more than half of the jurors where in tears as we gave accounts of our abuse.

It only took about 2 hours to deliberate and for the jury to come back ready to render a verdict; which could have been a very bad or good sign because that means they already had their minds made up. Once they announced a verdict has been reached and they were ready to deliver the fate of this sinister man; my family, myself and his other victims gathered in the court sitting side by side hand and hand with our faces looking towards the floor praying and waiting in suspense. The judge began reading off each charge….we held our breath.

In the case of C.M. vs. The State of Texas, we the jury find the defendant….
The entire court room fell silent and still, no one even moved until the sighs and screams filled the room, as the NOT GUILTY ON ALL COUNTS verdict was read.
I sat in the aisle for a few moments paralyzed, trying to process the bullshit I just heard.

That's it??!! This creep took our innocence, childhood and my mother's life and he gets away Scott free?! I ran out of the court room, pushing and knocking down anyone that stood in my way. I had to get out of there. The room felt as if it was closing in on me and I couldn't breathe; I was hyperventilating.

Camera crews chased us to our cars trying to get pictures and spitting out questions back to back, a million per second. "How do you feel?, Are you mad?, "Did you lie?" where the questions asked the most. We finally found our car through the crowd of people and media and then sped off as fast as the engine would allow.

I was awake that entire night trying to convince myself that it was all a terrible nightmare, but each time that thought came crashing down with the harsh reality that he was actually let go and we lost. The next morning came slowly, but now it was time to head back to Louisiana to try to pick up where we left off.

What started as a mission to help my oldest sister and the rest of us to heal from what happened in the past, but ended up hurting us more than it helped.

My oldest sister just found out her entire life was a lie and now had no idea who she truly was. Now being more confused than ever, she spiraled out of control, more than she was before the trial. Her drug use and reckless behavior increased, as her interest in living and taking care of her children decreased. With the plan to help her being an undeniable a failure, I had no choice but to continue to raise her children.

Months turned into years and I was still struggling mentally and financially, but was making it through school undisturbed and the kids were doing well. I tried to give them what they needed and to ease their minds when it came to missing their mom and understanding why she wasn't around. She would visit once, maybe twice every couple of months, any other time we would spot her was when she stood on the corner of the known crack house as I drove by and tried to prevent the kids from seeing.

Raising 2 kids while below the poverty was tough, especially when the kids weren't mine and I was regretting giving up my future in basketball. I was in misery, depressed and at the beginning stages of digging myself back in a hole. My relationship was short lived with the man I met in college. He had more issues than I did. He was very suicidal and he wasn't good for my life so I took the higher road and ended it.

Newly single and starting to revert back to my old ways and the only way I knew how to cope with my emotional pain. Thankfully, I was spared when I reunited with a man back home in Houston over the internet. We met playing basketball and haven't spoken in years and out of the blue we run into each other in a popular chat room. Maybe because I was vulnerable or just naïve, but through his charm and personality I fell in love. Another one of the biggest mistake of my life! At first, we had immediate chemistry and in my eyes he was the hottest thing since a summer in Houston, so I decided to take our relationship further.

I made it to my senior year, last semester of college and during this time, I would travel back and forth to Houston during our school breaks to visit him, which brought us closer. During my last semester of college life, 5 months before graduation the unthinkable happened. I never thought something like this would happen to me. I didn't want to slow down my lifestyle or share the spotlight with anyone, but 6 weeks after coming back to school from my visit with "Mr. Love Machine", I found out I was pregnant. I must say, he was far less than happy when I gave him the news. The last words I heard from his mouth before hanging up the phone in my face was, "It ain't mine". What have I gotten myself into...?

The pregnancy was the absolute worse experience of my life starting from the first trimester. Early in my pregnancy, I had a 'threatened miscarriage' in the middle of class, blood gushing down my leg and onto the floor, in front an auditorium full of students. A classmate rushed me to the hospital just for a doctor to tell me I had to be on bed rest for the next 3 months. Terrified I was going to lose my baby, I had to disobey the doctor's orders; I couldn't stay in bed, I still had 2 kids to care for and had to complete my last semester to graduate.

Growing bigger and bigger by the day I successfully made it to the end of the semester, and at the same time, the beginning of my 2nd trimester.

I did it!! I completed 4 years and was about to receive something no one in my family ever has, A Bachelor's Degree!!!

Knowing College Graduation this was supposed to be the best day of my life and a joyous occasion surrounded by supportive family, parties and balloons; the whole 9 yards for such an accomplishment, I was super excited for the celebration to come but instead, I was greeted with an eviction notice plastered on my door. My lease had expired and being 6 months pregnant and sick, I was unable to hold a job and unable to renew my lease; so now on top of all of that, I was homeless. I had nowhere to go and no one to turn to. I was hoping that when my family came to attend my graduation as they promised, since I was the only sibling to graduate from college, I could ask someone for help.

On graduation day, I waited for hours for my siblings and grandparents to arrive so we could car pool to the graduation and then a small celebration dinner following.

No one showed up for me at all; only my niece, nephew and the baby

I was carrying in my belly was there to witness me walk across the stage.

With this, I couldn't focus on the ceremony and my baby was doing flips in my uterus. I just wanted it to be over and to go home and cry; this was not the college graduation I envisioned. As we were leaving the arena, with my long sad face, I got a pleasant surprise when I notice my oldest sister was standing in the lobby waiting for us. Even though she was late and so drunk and high she was stumbling as she walked, I didn't even care; at least she showed up and was there for me for once.

Now that graduation was over, I had to face reality that I had no money, no job and now homeless and out on the streets at 6 months pregnant. Once evicted, I didn't have the means to rent a truck so I had a personal estate sale to try to make some change off of selling my belongings. At the end of the day, all I possessed was the clothes on my back and in a trash bag and $200 I collected to buy food and a motel room for as long as I could until I figured out what our next move should be.

I started to become very ill again, due to the stress and my blood pressure sky rocketed and hypertension set in. After 2 weeks, our food supply and shelter were gone. I was in full panic mode and at my wits end when I was sent the most unexpected blessing from the most unexpected person.

Around the time of my graduation, my oldest sister was living with one of the biggest drug dealers in the Northern parts of Louisiana, as his lady. This man turned things around for my sister. He kept her wearing nice clothes and hair done; not to mention an endless supply of cocaine.

I know what you are thinking, as a drug dealer and thug, this man had to have been a mean, cold blooded killer with a stone heart. Actually, on the contrary, he was one of the kindest, patient and most compassionate people that rescued me and the kids. He allowed my niece, nephew and me to live with him, even though he only anticipated for the stay to be for a few days.

Those few days passed pretty fast and I was faced with a dilemma of asking this man, that I just met, if we could extend our stay. When I fully explained my situation and seeing my full, pregnant belly, he insisted we stay at his home as long we needed to figure out what was the next step in my life.

This man didn't live in a big, fancy house, as a matter of fact, he lived in one of the most dangerous neighborhoods in the city, and yet, I felt more safe and protected with him. Everyone knew not to mess with Mr. DJ or his people and he had his own personal security that would keep watch outside.

I made sure I did my part while living under his roof. My duties consisted of cleaning the quarters the kids and I slept in, the kitchen, the bathroom and washed and fold the dirty laundry. I was more than happy to perform those duties, for the kindness that this man had bestowed upon me without reason.

Mr. DJ and my sister would argue constantly how she needed to started to do more around the house and I could tell that my sister was wearing out her welcome rather quickly. I tried my best to stay out of Mr. DJ's way and help out as much as I physically could. Even if that meant, sitting outside, on the porch for a couple of hours while he cooked up a batch of his work, homemade cocaine; which smelled like burning plastic.

The most amusing aspect of Mr. DJ was that he rocked a 1980's Jerry Curl and always had on a suite with the matching shoes. He had that super Old School Style, very sharp and smooth and all of the ladies in town wanted to be his. The most surprising detail about him, he was a Deacon of his congregation and a faithful member of the church choir. This man had irony written all over his face.

Without pause, my 2 week anniversary of moving in with Mr. DJ and my sister was approaching and so was the end of my last trimester. The arguing between my sister and Mr. DJ had been escalating within the weeks I lived with them and naturally I thought it was because of me. Although he hadn't said anything to me about leaving, maybe he just didn't want to upset a pregnant lady so far along with his wishes. So one day after one of their biggest arguments, I went and asked my sister what they were fighting about. She looked me dead in my eyes and said that Mr. DJ wanted me to leave because I was too much of a burden on him and the household. I didn't see this coming by a long shot, but now, back in panic mode, I had to find another place to stay and according to my sister, ASAP. Before leaving, I tried to find Mr. DJ to ask him what I had done to be asked to leave so abruptly. I was unable to catch him before he left for church, but my sister warned me not to approach him or I would see the side of him that everyone feared.

Distraught, I gathered what I had left, said goodbye to my niece and nephew, loaded my Ford Taurus and headed away from his house with no destination in mind. My gas tank was on E, so I couldn't go very far, but my spirit guided me to my ex-boyfriend's mom's house. I didn't know many people and she lived close to Mr. DJ's house so I decided to take a chance. When I first arrived, I was shocked to see a U-Haul truck in their drive-way; finding out that they were just evicted as well and had to move in with in-laws; so that plan was a bust. My major advantage that came from my detour to her house was that I ran into my ex-boyfriend for the first time in months and he promised to help me anyway he could. I could tell he felt sorry for me. He would sneak me food out of his relatives frig, and made sure I at least had something to eat. Since I had nowhere to go, as the night was drawing near, I decided to park and spend the night in the hospital parking just in case I went into early labor.

Within the next couple of day, the Louisiana summer heat had gotten so hot, the letters on one of my shirts left in my car melted off. With having no AC in my car, I nor my unborn would last another day in those highly, elevated temperatures.

Scared to death of his reaction, but facing certain death from heat stroke or the death of my child, I had no choice but to confront Mr. DJ to see if I could resolve the reason he had thrown me out. I was desperate. I sat in his drive way rehearsing what I would say and how carefully I would say it, making sure I don't make him explode on me like he done to so many others. I took a few deep breaths, rubbed my belly for luck, said a prayer and starting walking towards the backyard where I heard his voice traveling from. While walking along side of his house, I saw my sister in the window, violently shaking her head, gesturing for me to leave. Determined, hungry and hot as hell, there was nothing she could do or say to stop me. My footsteps started to slow once I saw his Jerry Curl glisten in the sun. I made sure my face looked extra sad as I approached.

I thought once he spotted me back at his house after he told me to leave, he was going to start screaming and cursing, but once he saw me it was nothing like that. His seemed peaceful and he smiled as he waved for me to come over to where he was sitting. "Hey Baby girl", he greeted me and asked if I needed something to eat or drink. Shocked by his concerned demeanor, I was even more curious as to why I had to leave; so now with less fear, I asked him.

He stood dumb founded for a second and this is when the fear started to creep back inside of me. He called my sister to come outside and asked her what she told me. I didn't give her a chance to speak, when I blurted out everything that was said. Mr. DJ let me know that everything my sister told me was a lie.

All of their arguing was because she felt threatened that Mr. DJ kept comparing my sister to me with how I helped around the house. That's all she needed to hear before she plotted to get me out of there.

Even though I was welcomed by Mr. DJ, I decided to find another place to stay, but this time I needed a stable place because I was going to give birth in a short amount of time. A recent college graduate, with no further ties to Louisiana, I orchestrated a plan to move back to Houston.

Even though I didn't want to ask her, my 2nd oldest sister just moved into a house with her boyfriend and they had more than enough space and I could help her with her toddler to save them money on daycare expenses. I was worried because the last time we spoke was before the graduation disappointment.

Honestly I didn't care too much about that at this point because I had to find another place to stay until my little one arrived. If she agreed to let me move back to Houston, to reside with her and her family, I would have to figure out how I was going to make it 400 miles back to Houston. My car was on its last leg and wasn't in the condition to make it all the way back. I surely didn't want to be stranded in the middle of nowhere, almost 8 months pregnant.

By the grace of God, my sister in Houston agreed to allow me to travel back to Houston to stay with her until I delivered my baby. Mr. DJ had one of most loyal crack head customers that so happened to be a mechanic, inspect my car and do any minor fixes he could. The only payment I had to come up with was a 6-pack of beer and a pack of cigarettes for his services.

Being worried about traveling so far alone and so pregnant, my ex-boyfriend offered to drive down to Houston with me to make sure I arrived safely and then take the Grey Hound bus back to Louisiana and Mr. DJ gave me money for gas and food. . It was all set, I was about to head back to the place I worked so hard to get away from.

With the sun setting and the cool night breeze, the 5 hour drive was very relaxing knowing I had somewhere to go. We arrived in Houston around 3 a.m. and with a sense of relief and that stress eliminated, I passed out exhausted from the trip. I'm sure my ex-boyfriend didn't get much rest knowing in the morning he will be leaving Houston, not knowing the next time or if he will ever see me again.

It was a sad departure when my sister and I dropped him off at the bus station the next morning. We hugged each other for such a long period before he boarded with tears in our eyes and a tremble in our voices. Not wanting to let each other go and give up the years that we spent together, he stepped on the Grey Hound and I watched him pull off and out of my life for good. While watching him leave, I reflected on how our relationship ended, I felt extremely guilty and horrible knowing that I crushed this man's heart with the break-up and my unexpected pregnancy from another man. Regardless of his mental issues, he genuinely loved me and that is very hard to find; Lesson Learned.

It took me a couple of days to recover and get fully rested from everything that had transpired the days prior. My sister, her boyfriend and I, officially agreed in exchange for room and board, I would babysit my 3 year old niece while they went to work as long as I lived with them. It was a sweet deal; they had a big house, internet, cable and all of the food and snacks I could eat. Plus I was home all day alone, with their baby girl, for 8 hours each day; no stress and as much rest as I can get in the last weeks of my pregnancy.

Now back in Houston, I was starting to wrap my head around the reality of my situation. I was 8 months pregnant, broke and head over hills in love with this asshole that won't acknowledge I am carrying his child. Consumed with my own issues, I forgot about my 2nd oldest sister's cocaine and pill addiction and had no clue of how bad it had gotten after she moved back from Houston from living with me in Louisiana for a short period of time during the trial.

She and her boyfriend would get into knock down drag out fights because she would come home at early hours of the morning geeked up on Cocaine or obnoxiously drunk with only a few hours before she was to leave for work, not knowing where she had been the entire night. Her behavior had gotten very erratic once she gained employment at a Pain Management Clinic; her addiction became out of control. She would steal pill samples from her job and even went as far as stealing a doctor's prescription tablet in an attempt to write her own prescriptions.

With the drug use, her attitude towards me was so unpredictable and fierce, we would get into screaming matches and physical altercations because on her drug binges, she felt the need to express her disapproval of my pregnancy, saying the most hurtful, disrespectful words she could think of. These occurrences didn't happen too often; her boyfriend wasn't having it and was the mediator between us concerned for my well-being, but when they did happen, they were explosive.

One of the problems with us. young, single mothers, is the fact that we tend to cling to the sperm donors, thinking just because I was having his baby, he would completely change and act the way, I feel, a father is supposed to. At first, once back in Houston, he seemed to be adamant about not wanting to be in my unborn child's or my life. At 8 months pregnant, he came to visit me one time for 15 minutes when I made it back and then avoided me for the next 5 weeks. My dreams for a family with the perfect man was fading right in front of my eyes. I thought for sure since his 4 year old son passed away 2 weeks after finding out I was pregnant, he would want to be there every step of the way, but I was dead wrong. He eventually started coming to visit more often, but only during late, booty call hours and just to have sex then leave. This sexual charade went on until I was about to go into labor and then once again he went M.I.A

I was in the hospital for 2 days in labor and didn't even receive neither a phone call, nor a visit from him. My sister and her boyfriend were the only ones there when I went into labor and once my little girl made her debut to the world at 7lbs 5oz, my sister was the one that cut the umbilical cord and took the pictures of my daughter entering the world with all my shining glory. It was a very nice moment that my sister and I shared. For once, she wasn't drunk or high; and knowing we didn't get along growing up, but this was an experience that only we would always share. Not knowing how important this bonding experience was going to be between her and me, but within the next 3 weeks would prove to be monumental.

Three days after having my baby, I was back at home starting my life as a new mommy. After the first 2 weeks, I swore never to have another one EVER AGAIN. She cried and cried for hours with nothing that seemed to soothe her. One top of the constant crying, sleepless night, and painful constipation; I was breast feeding, that was an experience in itself.

Eventually her father showed up one day to see her and my stupid ass fell right back in to the illusion of having the happy mother, father and baby family life, something I wanted so dearly for myself and child; what I never had. I gave my daughter his last name and a full name that would give them both the same initials; trying to do something special to make him feel a part of her. Thankfully, he started coming around more, still during late night hours, but in my mind, any time is better than none at all.

With the help of my sister and her boyfriend, I was feeling better from minimal hours of sleep, the crying and every other annoying thing an unborn dishes out. My mind wasn't stuck on trying to win the love of my daughter's father any longer or the drama and fighting going on in the house, my only concern now was the little ball of skin in my arms. Maybe if my mind wasn't so wrapped up in myself, I would have been able to stop the tragedy yet to come.

In the middle of the night, my sister and her boyfriend ignited one of their usual brawls and my sister charged out of the house in a fit a rage and didn't return for about 4 hours give or take. You could smell the stench of alcohol on her breath from the driveway and obviously high out of her mind off of something strong. I was sitting on the stairs next to the front door, holding my newborn when she stammered in, paced slowly over to where I was sitting, reached out her arms signaling she wanted to hold the. With close assistance, I allowed my sister to hold my baby hoping it would make her feel better from the argument. She held the baby and starred deep in her eyes for about 2 minutes, handed her back to me and the proceeded to leave out of the house once again. I begged her to stay and to sleep if off because it wasn't safe for her to be out at night alone, in the condition she was in, driving. She barely even acknowledge my request as she continued to walk out of the door. I honestly expected her to come back in the house fairly quickly because my sister was a drama queen and always made elaborate attempts to capture her boyfriend's attention, but this time was different.

My sister wondered back home around 3 a.m. and creeped up the stairs so her boyfriend wouldn't hear her. She found her way to my room and was barely able to stand and slurring her words, asked my daughters father for ride to work in the morning because her car was towed and she didn't want to tell her boyfriend in fear of his reaction. As she tried to stand normally waiting for his answer, I was laughing, watching her try to hold herself steady while sliding down the door hinge. The drugs that she had taken was making her go in and out of being asleep and responsive.
In retrospect, it wouldn't have been so funny if I would have known that this was going to be my last time talking to my sister ever again.

That very morning, only a few hours after she came home, I went into my niece's room, where my sister crashed out for the night, right across the hall from me, to wake her up for work. When I entered the room, it was freezing cold as the window A/C unit was blasting at 55 degrees and was she completely naked and uncovered. I was startled when I heard a loud, growling snore coming from her nose. I shook her a few times and called out her name trying to wake her up with no response. Maybe she was just in a deep sleep; she was really drunk and high and could need a little time to sleep it off. Louder, I called her name a few more times and shook her violently trying to get her to respond in some type of way. I started getting very nervous when I noticed the tip of her fingers were turning a blueish color and wrinkled, like when you sit in water for too long.

I ran downstairs as quickly as my episiotomy stiches allowed, to notify her boyfriend. He immediately jumped out of bed and bolted up the stairs to his girlfriend's side. He made several attempts to wake her up and stated if she didn't respond in the next 15 minutes, we would put her in the tube of cold water, as he normally did when she was passed out, to get her to wake up. As her boyfriend was preparing the cold shower, I placed my baby monitor next to my sister's head to make sure I could still hear her breathing when I had to leave her unsupervised to tend to my new born. Within 5 minutes, after I left the room to breastfeed, I heard her boyfriend screaming for me to call the ambulance. Our worst fears came true; my sister stopped breathing.
I ran in the room, called 911, we drug her freezing cold, limp body off of the bed onto the floor and I starting performing CPR on her.

Frantically trying to give her CPR, while trying to breathe life back into her body and resuscitate her, I had to pause between each set of chest compressions trying to avoid throwing up everything in my stomach. Apparently, my sister had eaten garlic chicken wings for dinner that night, so when giving her mouth to mouth, garlic foam shot out of her throat and into my mouth causing me to gag intensely.

It seems to take hours for the ambulance to arrive, but when we heard the sirens, my sister's boyfriend and his best friend carried her lifeless body down the stairs so the paramedics could quickly reach her because at this point she has been without oxygen for almost 15 minutes. Once the paramedics took over I rushed to search for her work bag looking for any clues to what she may have ingested that night. I thought that if they knew what was in her system, they would have a better chance of saving her. I ended up giving them 4 different pill bottles of the strongest medicine on the market, intended for cancer patients, a bag of cocaine and bottles of Vodka.

Her 3 year old woke up from the commotion and I rushed to cover her eyes to prevent her from seeing her mommy on the floor naked, with men forcing tubes down her throat. I turned on her favorite cartoon to calm her and by time I exited the room, my sister was in the ambulance heading to the hospital.

Following behind the ambulance, we arrived at the hospital in record time; running lights and swerving in traffic, dodging cars gave me a flash back of us rushing to the hospital when my mother was killed. "Please Lord, not again", I remember thinking, while driving like a bat of out of hell. Upon arrival, to the same hospital that I delivered my daughter at 3 weeks earlier, we were directed to the same floor I gave birth.

We waited in the lobby for hours waiting on her status. While I was busy making and responding to phone calls, I had to sneak away every 3 hours to find a handicap restroom or stall to breast feed my newborn.

Once the doctor walked in the waiting room to inform us of her prognosis, all hope for her survival had been crushed. He took me into a side room and explained that every single organ in her body had shut down simultaneously due to ingesting so many chemicals at one time, better known as an overdose.

The next words out of the doctor's mouth made every single hair on my body stand up and I broke down without warning. "Her body is a catastrophe" were the last words I heard before he asked me to make one of the toughest decisions that anyone should ever have to make. The same heart wrenching decision that had to be made one time before in my life; whether to pull the plug or leave her on life support with less than a 10% chance of survival.

Already suffering from post-partum depression, it was difficult for me to process what I was being asked to do and I damn sure wasn't in any mental condition to decide whether to give up on my sisters life or not. I was silently talking to my sister and praying that I wouldn't have to make this ultimate decision. No later than my AMEN, the machines my sister was connected to started going berserk and alarms blaring; her heart had stopped and she flat lined. The doctors rushed in, shoving me out of the room so they could use the defibrillator and get her heart back beating. The doctors were successful with bringing her back to life, but her pulse was still very weak. Within the hour, her heart gave out 2 more times and that's when the doctor's felt it necessary to call her time of death. And just like that, my sister was dead.

In disbelief, I stood next to my sister lying lifeless, with her extremely swollen face from her biting off her tongue during a convulsion she had before her heart stopped the first time. I stood petrified in one spot for so long without movement, knees locked, I felt the blood leaving my legs while it rushed to the top of my head. My nose started bleeding profusely and I got very light headed. The next thing I know, the doctors were rushing over to me and I was flat on my back looking straight up at the ceiling. I gathered my strength to pick myself up off of the floor, the doctors checked my vitals and helped me make my way back over to my sister's bed to say my final goodbyes. All I could do, as grief rushed over me, was to hold her hand as her skin became colder and colder, bury my face into the side of her bed and cry, devastated.

I didn't sleep for days after my sister died. Every time I was in bed I could hear her footsteps coming up the stairs or her voice calling my name from the bottom of the stairs. I would break down every time my niece would come home, rush to my sister's room and just stand in the doorway starring into the darkness, hoping her mommy would invite her in to come and jump on the bed as she usually would. My nieces face would drop every single day after realizing her mommy wasn't there in the darkness waiting for her and too young to understand why she was gone. All she knew and could feel was that mommy wasn't coming home; a feeling I knew all too well.

Here we go once again, funeral arrangements had to be made and with no money to make them. My oldest sister traveled back to Houston from Louisiana, were she was still living with Mr. DJ, to help with the plans. No life insurance or savings we had no idea how we were to pay for my sister's services. We had one week to raise $6000 for her funeral and burial with exactly $0 to our names. We quickly found out who her true friends were because all of my sister's "so-called" best friends and people that claimed to love her dearly wouldn't even answer the phone when we called. No one even called to offer any donations, condolences flowers...nothing! We literally called over 200 people and could barely find anyone that would help us bury our sister. The funeral coordinator even threatened to cancel the funeral if we didn't have the entire balance paid by the deadline. My oldest sister and I, with only a few hours to spare before the viewing of the body, hustled up every penny, nickel and dime we could until it was paid in full.

Everything had fallen into place at the last possible second and now it was time to lay our sister to rest.

Like my mother, my sister looked like a completely different person in the casket. Her prolonged drug use totally destroyed what she once was. Her face was still swollen 2 times its original size and her nose was sunk into her face, practically gone. Death had stolen her beauty.

There was a very small number of people in attendance and only 1 of her closest friends was there. Even my brother was so distraught and couldn't bring himself to see our sister in a coffin, so he didn't come.

After an hour of listening to a sermon, last words and prayers the funeral service was finally over and we had an hour drive from the church to the cemetery for the burial. Shockingly, my 1 month old stayed asleep the entire procession, but to add to the misery, it started pouring down the freezing November rain, and woke her up. So while the final thoughts and burial was taking place at the cemetery, I had to stay in the car to breastfeed and to keep her warm from the dropping temperature and bad weather. I watched the casket lowered into the ground from the car window and a final prayer was said. "Good Bye Sis".

The following days after the funeral were very hectic with everyone trying to put their lives back together, not knowing where to start. Since my sister had died in the house we were living in, my sister's boyfriend was, understandably, having difficulties staying there, so he decided to move and find a more suitable place for him and his grief stricken 3 year old.

I was homeless and desperate once again, but the difference is now I had a little life with me, plus postpartum depression and grief to get under control.

I did the only thing I could do, I went to my daughter's father's family for help. His mother didn't even know about the baby and was delighted to welcome her new grandchild since she just lost one months' earlier. She helped me out tremendously during my time of need, but with her being from another country in Africa, she had her own issues, very strong opinions and was very controlling, so we had many altercations and I had to keep my distance.

Time passed by and it would be years of me trying to learn my purpose and what I was supposed to do with my life. Working 2 or more jobs at a time, bouts of homelessness to where I would sleep in the back of my vehicle and leave my daughter with her grandmother while I was studying and looking for work, horrible relationship choices with men that would rob, steal, beat and cheat on me; life didn't seem to letting up on me.

I had to watch my brother get addicted to pills and go to prison for years on charges of Armed Robbery and oldest sister relapse time and time again on cocaine and pills, moving closer and closer to death if she couldn't grab ahold of her addiction.

This was one of the lowest points in my life I was looking for a lifeline; some type of support and guidance. Ironically, that lifeline would come in the form of my daughter's grandmother. She convinced me to use my Bachelor's Degree to go back to school to earn my Teaching Certificate after years of failed corporate ventures.

I am now an elementary Physical Education/Adaptive Physical Education Teacher with a stable life, but still fighting to maintain my sanity. Life is still a struggle and I am still learning how to manage my emotions and memories of my past.

I always felt my family was cursed and thought maybe the universe was punishing us for my mother's choices or maybe because of a past life, but maybe just maybe, I am the one that made it out for a greater purpose. But one thing is certain, the way life has been treating us thus far, I'm sure I will find out what that is sooner than later. But life goes on...

Made in the USA
Coppell, TX
17 September 2022